CRITICAL CONDITION:

women on the edge of violence

EDITED BY AMY SCHOLDER

CITY LIGHTS BOOKS / SAN FRANCISCO

Cover design & photography by Rex Ray
Book design by Rex Ray and Amy Scholder

Library of Congress Cataloging-in-Publication Data

Critical condition: women on the edge of violence / edited by Amy Scholder.
p. cm.
ISBN 0-87286-285-2 : $10.95
      1. Women—United States—Crimes against—Literary collections. 2. Violence—
United States—Literary collections. 3. Women—United States—Crimes against. 4. American
literature—Women authors. 5. American literature—20th century. 6. Violence—United States.
7. Violence in art. 8. Women in art. I. Scholder, Amy.
PS509.W6C75 1993
                                    810.9'352042—dc20   93-5565
                                                                          CIP

Poems by Wanda Coleman: "Sapphire as Artist in the World," Sex and Politics in Fairyland," "Chair
Affair," "Confessions Noires," and "Of Apes and Men" copyright ©1993 by Wanda Coleman,
reprinted from *Hand Dance.* "Fat Lena" copyright ©1988 by Wanda Coleman, reprinted from *A War
of Eyes and Other Stories.* "No Woman's Land" copyright ©1979 by Wanda Coleman reprinted from
African Sleeping Sickness: Stories & Poems. "Rape" copyright ©1983 by Wanda Coleman, reprinted
from *Imagoes.* All poems reprinted with the permission of Black Sparrow Press.

Poems by Sapphire ©1993 by Sapphire, from *American Dreams: Poetry & Prose,* forthcoming from
HIGH RISK Books/Serpent's Tail, 1994.

City Lights Books are available to bookstores through our primary distributor: Subterranean
Company, PO Box 160, 265 S. 5th Street, Monroe, OR 97456. 503-847-5274. Toll free orders
800-274-7826. FAX 503-847-6018. Our books are also available through library jobbers and
regional distributors. For personal orders and catalogs, please write to City Lights Books, 261
Columbus Avenue, San Francisco, CA 94133.

CITY LIGHTS BOOKS are edited by Lawrence Ferlinghetti and Nancy J. Peters and published at the
City Lights Bookstore, 261 Columbus Avenue, San Francisco, CA 94133.

10 9 8 7 6 5 4 3 2

CONTENTS

VISUAL ART

Acknowledgements

Many thanks to Zoey Kroll, my editorial assistant; Laura Brün; Margaret Crane; Nancy J. Peters; Julia Wong; Keesje Fischer; Brad Trayser; Women's Work, Liz Claiborne, Inc; and Rex Ray. And to all the artists, writers and activists who participated in the events highlighted here, and who brought forward their stories and ideas with hope and fearlessness, from which I learned a great deal.
—A.S.

In America today, women are on the edge of violence.

Every 15 seconds a woman is assaulted and beaten.

4,000,000 women a year are assaulted by their male partners.

Every day, 4 women are murdered by husbands or boyfriends.

A woman is raped every 1.3 minutes.

61% of all rapes are of women under 17 years old.
29% of all rapes are of women under 11 years old.

1 out of 8 Hollywood films have a rape motif.

92% of women in prison [in the last 10 years] had less than
$10,000 a year income.

80% of women in prison have children.

Prison terms for killing husbands are twice as long as for killing wives.

93% of women who killed their mates had been battered by them.
67% killed them to protect themselves and their children at the moment of murder.

25% of all crime is wife assault.

60% of all battered women are beaten while they are pregnant.

70% of men who batter their wives sexually or physically abuse their children.

38% of women have been abused sexually by an adult relative,
acquaintance or stranger before they are 18;
28% before the age 14.

16% of men have been abused sexually as children.

The amount spent to shelter animals is three times the amount spent to provide
emergency shelter to women from domestic violence situations.

Domestic violence is the number one cause of emergency room visits by women.

Sources: *WAC Stats: The Facts about Women* (The New Press, 1993); Women's Work Program, Liz Claiborne, Inc.

Two articles appeared today in the *San Francisco Chronicle*. The front page featured a color photo and prominent story about the slaying of Kristy Ramsey by Gordon Kimbrough. She was knifed and strangled to death. "Kimbrough was apparently angered over her intention to end the couple's often-stormy love affair." The article goes on to focus on his use of steroids and apparent connection to an illegal anabolic steroid prescription scheme; the police officer who knew Kimbrough from the gym and rushed to the scene to talk him out of killing himself; and, the couple's "stormy" history of violence and various police complaints that he filed against other lovers. Couched in this report (following two quotes: "She was like an angel, and he was a real gentleman"; and, ". . . [he's] a big teddy bear of a guy who views himself as a ladies man") was the fact that he was known to have beaten her. A police officer wrote a report in October, 1992: "Ramsey told me that Kimbrough had hit her on prior occasions but she had not contacted the police." A man who knew Kimbrough for thirteen years said, "He'd been known to knock her around . . . "

This story made the headlines not because of the murder of this woman, or their "stormy" relationship in which he battered her, but because of the steroid/male-bodybuilding angle. The article mentions "roid rage," which typically accompanies long-term use of steroids, and one man suggested that Kimbrough's use of steroids could be used to *help* him with his defense, since "it makes you very testy and you can fly into a rage."

For anyone familiar with patterns of abuse, this story is a tragic demonstration of some of the most basic realities concerning women and violence. It exemplifies the unspeakably common occurence of domestic violence (an estimated 4 million women a year are savagely beaten by their partners; more than half the female murder victims in the US in 1991 were slain by their husbands or boyfriends); the fact that 75% of the women whose lives are threatened or taken happens when they are trying to leave or have already left

1

the relationship; and, the media's blindness to women who are trapped in these cycles of violence.

Critical Condition collects highlights from a conference called Feminism, Activism & Art which focused on women and violence. It also features performance texts and poetry presented in this context; visual art that deals with issues of women and power, and art that promotes public awareness of domestic violence and child abuse.

As organizers of the conference, we were shocked to discover that, given a general topic of Women and Violence, the participants focused almost exclusively, without any prompting on our parts, and without consulting one another, on the issues of incest, rape, domestic violence, and the price women pay for defending themselves. We found that we couldn't open a discussion of women who kill or commit violent acts without there being a discussion of wife-beating and self-defense. We couldn't raise issues of the media or of images of women in popular culture without confronting discriminatory values that determine whether women's lives (or deaths) qualify as newsworthy.

In response, the women included in *Critical Condition* challenge the dominant order of abuse and invisibility with powerful literary and visual art. They put a spin on issues of women and violence by focusing on women who fight back, some of whom kill their abusers; women who control their own sexualities and challenge conventional ideas of sex; women who assert images of themselves in a cultural landscape where none appear; women who reframe personal histories that were meant to shame them into oblivion.

The other article—"Man's Penis Reattached After Wife Cut it Off"— also appeared in the *San Francisco Chronicle* on June 24, 1993. (While my mentioning this article might fulfill a certain stereotype of a lesbian, ice-pick and all, I nonetheless want to point out a few things in the context of *Critical Condition*.) The fact that the woman in this story was raped and very probably feared for her own safety (the last sentence reads, almost as a postscript:

Man's Penis Reattached After Wife Cut it Off

Washington Post

Manassas, Va.

A man whose wife cut off his penis with a kitchen knife while he slept was in satisfactory condition at a hospital last night after 9½ hours of surgery to reattach the organ, officials said.

Authorities learned of the incident when the 28-year-old man showed up at a hospital about 5 a.m.

About the same time, a 24-year-old woman called authorities from a pay phone to say she had been raped by her husband, had fled their apartment "in a panic," unknowingly taking the penis with her, and had thrown it out the window of her car at an intersection.

The penis was recovered at the intersection, packed in ice and taken to Prince William Hospital, in Manassas, where Doctors James T. Sehn and David Berman reattached it. "We're hopeful the graft will be successful," Sehn said. "But we're still in a wait-and-see mode" for at least the next 24 hours.

The woman told police her husband raped her shortly before she cut off two-thirds of his penis. She was released after being treated as a rape victim at the same hospital where her husband was undergoing surgery.

Police charged her with aggravated malicious wounding, a felony that carries a maximum penalty of 40 years in jail. Prosecutor Paul Ebert said that police have been unable to interview the man and that no charges have been brought in connection with the rape allegation.

Ebert said the couple, who were not identified, "had been experiencing considerable domestic difficulty." Former neighbors said the woman had often complained of being beaten by her husband.

3

"Former neighbors said the woman had often complained of being beaten by her husband") is clearly not the relevant point in the coverage of this story. And, in as much as the media—and certainly this man—are completely unconcerned with the violence against her and her rights, this story further demonstrates the ways in which women's bodies are deemed violable, while violence against a man's body is of universal interest. Of course, I found myself indifferent to the success of his graft, while quite anxious about her fate at the hands of the justice system.

At first, I thought it was absurd that the nation's major newspapers publish stories I expect to find in the tabloids. But, then I considered the number of questions this kind of sensationalistic journalism provokes. And while I don't credit the *Washington Post* (where this article first appeared) or the *Chronicle* with these motivations, I keep hoping that readers will eventually wonder why so many lurid stories have at their core the abuse of women by their partners. I wonder, when will stories like this be reported differently, so that the woman's well-being is a subject for our concern and sympathy? When will women, who find themselves in situations similar to those reported in the media, learn from these ariticles how to escape potential violence? And, will stories about women who fight back ever act as a deterence to violence against women?

Working on this project, I have been haunted by the number of times I've been made aware of violence against women that goes virtually unchal-lenged in the world, and is often reaffirmed in mass media and popular culture. The reaction of the US Government, and every other government, against the systematic rape of Muslim women in Bosnia is perhaps a litmus test of humanity and how women are regarded in our civilization. How bleak and shameful that is.

As feminists have been saying for decades, the notion of a universal subject in American culture is still implicitly male. And, while there has been a new wave of feminism for the '90s, it has been staged against a backdrop of male hysteria, best summarized by the thinly veiled conservatism of the Men's Movement.

And yet, there are women artists and activists who have been chipping away at this dominant paradigm with fierce commitment and total irreverence. More than two dozen women artists, writers and activists in *Critical Condition* focus on the many questions of individual freedom and social justice. Their backgrounds and approaches are as diverse as they are personal. And the key to understanding a feminism for the '90s might be this display of work and discussion that goes beyond issues of survival on to an agenda of artistic freedom, sexual power, and self-determination.

MWI—
Many Women Involved

MWI—MANY WOMEN INVOLVED

A Performance Monologue by Carla Kirkwood

MWI is the performance component of the *NHI—No Humans Involved* public art project, presented in San Diego, February-March 1992. The project utilized billboards, a gallery installation, performance, a book, and panel discussions to examine this series of gender-motivated crimes. The *NHI* project is a collaboration of five artists: Deborah Small, Elizabeth Sisco, Carla Kirkwood, Scott Kessler, and Louis Hock.

Since 1985 at least forty-five women have been sexually assaulted and brutally murdered in San Diego County. These women have been labeled with the police term NHI (No Humans Involved). NHI is an in-house term used to discount crimes against individuals from marginalized sectors of society. In some of these murders the police themselves have been implicated.

7

MWI—Many Women Involved

I lay in the chair in front of the television. I didn't move. The heat in my arm and head knocked me out. I was on fire. The needle marks from the small pox vaccination were pounding on my upper left arm. The needle holes had started to crust over with small, watery blisters. I wanted to pick them, scratch them, but I wasn't allowed. The school nurse had lined us all up in the auditorium and carefully punched thirty to forty holes in every kid's arm. "Now some of you may feel a little feverish, but it will disappear in a day or two." It left a scar, a mark on my generation, the last to be pricked and poked. The news was on. I didn't care. Whenever I would wake up, the TV noises sounded like they were miles away. Barely audible. Strange sounds. I felt sick to my stomach and the Milky Way bar my mom had stuffed in my left hand was beginning to melt from the heat. She always gave me candy, chocolate, whenever I felt bad. Our greatest moments came from sharing chocolate bars. "Sis, why don't you run down and get us some candy?" Then she'd open her coin purse and pull out change for two bars. "Here, get a Hershey bar for me and whatever you want for yourself. And when you get back take a bath, you need a bath, honey." She always said that. She always told me to take a bath, even when I wasn't dirty. I felt something wet in my ear. A finger or tongue moving its way through the canals of my ear. Without consent. Like whispering. The idea that you are sharing a secret, being a participant. I hated that feeling. He always did it. Grandpa, reading in my ear, biting it when no one was in the room.

Then it stopped and I could feel the moisture dry up on the skin. A minute later the same thing happened, then somebody laughed. It wasn't him. It was Sharon, my cousin. She laughed again. "Did you see that?" she said, pointing at the television. "Don't do that, you know how I hate it, don't do that. I don't feel good." She knew why I felt that way. Then she said, louder, puffing on a menthol cigarette, "Did you see that?" She'd keep it up until I said something. "What?" I

8

said. "She's dead." "What?" "She's dead." "Who's dead?" "They found her in the riverbed, the Tijuana riverbed."

All those news reports, searching, images of family crying, a high school photo. It was over. Over in away I hadn't expected. Over in a way that threatened everything. It gave me a knowledge, a knowledge that was dangerous. I knew who she was, every girl in my elementary school knew who she was. Years later, friends I had gone to school with would remember this case, even her first name, Mary Lou. It changed how we felt about the world. At the time everybody's mom was nervous. I wasn't supposed to play outside by myself anymore, not after sundown. No more. Somebody was out there. Sharon licked my ear again and laughed. I told her to stop it. She said, "Isn't that something? Her being dead like that."

It was something. Nothing had ever happened like this before. First time. San Diego was a quiet little town. Everybody was shocked. She was a junior from Hilltop High in Chula Vista. Her picture was in every newspaper. For two weeks, people combed the area looking for her, for any sign of her. Mary Lou Olsen. Cheerleader. Sweet-faced. Disappeared, fourteen days ago. "She was raped." Sharon got serious. "They raped her and strangled her, and then stuffed blue rags down her throat. You know, the kind of blue paper rags they wash your windshield with at the gas station. They just dumped her like a sack of potatoes." I didn't want to hear anymore. I wanted them to find her, hiding out at some friend's house, mad at her parents. Maybe at Belmont Park, hiding inside one of the closed rides, merry-go-round, bumper cars, fun house. Sharon started to lick me again, and I yelled at her to get away. She knew what it meant, how I hated it. How creepy it was that he would do that to me, and to her. He always treated us like we were making him evil, crazy, teasing him with this thing we had. He owned us. We had something that was his. Keeping it from him. He had to have it, it was his right.

9

She knew better than to lick me like that. "I'm sorry," she said. "I shouldn't kid around with you like that, sorry." I told her about the fever, that I didn't feel good and she helped me up and into the bedroom. She lay next to me and started talking about Mary Lou. "I wonder if Grandpa did it? What do you think?" Then she laughed. I told her to shut up. I didn't want to talk about it. And, no, I didn't think Grandpa did it. "Yeah you're right, lots of people could have done it." I didn't believe that. I pictured a monster, a gang of maniacs, screaming, with big red eyes, those gangs of monsters that hide in corners late at night. I wanted to cry, but I didn't. I was scared. Now, going outside would never feel like being free, like being safe from the inside, safe from this house. They never found who did it. No one was arrested or tried or sentenced. Unsolved. Years later a girlfriend of mine told me how it always bothered her that no one was ever caught. "Somebody got away with murder," she said. "And they're still out there somewhere." There were rumors that the police might have been involved, that she was seen near a car.

10

Sharon rolled over close to me and said that I shouldn't worry about it. I was a good girl, no matter what. But, I thought, Mary Lou was a good girl, a cheerleader, her parents loved her. They were on the TV almost every night asking people to help them find their little girl. Sharon said it was a once in a lifetime thing. "You're a good girl, nothing like that will ever happen to you, it won't. I'd kill anybody that hurt you." She meant it. She really meant it. Grandpa used to say that I was a good girl, too. Talking like a preacher, teaching me things to remember all my life. The lesson. Sorting out, dividing, separating off, the good from the bad, the valuable from the less valuable. Me and Sharon and him—a miniature of the whole world. He said that Sharon wasn't so good, Sharon did things with men that she shouldn't do. Grandpa said that there was something about her that made men act a certain way. Made him act a certain way. Grandpa always said that he was one of the few good people in the world, evil was outside of him, all around him, tempting him. He would talk to me like a teacher, instructing me. "Good girls never tell." The lesson. Things to remember, all the days of my life. Me and Sharon and him. But I knew what he did to Sharon. I knew that he was the first one. Nothing he could say would separate her from me. "Some women just drive men crazy," he would say. "They know what they have between their legs and they drive men crazy with it. Your cousin, she's like that. But you're not, you're a good girl." Then he'd look at me for a long time. "What you got down there, sweetheart, right down there in the middle of your legs?" And he would point down at my skirt and lift it up with his foot. "You're a good girl, not like your cousin."

Sharon pulled the covers over us and put her arm around me. I felt safe. She was the only person who knew everything and who would protect me. Everybody in the family talked about what she did with men, and that she did it for money. They'd sit around the TV news at night and comment on the latest news about Mary Lou. What a tragedy it was, such a nice girl. And how her parents seemed like such nice people. The parents had given the police a full description of what she was wearing the night she disappeared, good girl clothes. When they found her, all she had left was the top portion of her blouse, wound around her neck. My mom reminded Sharon that if she wasn't more careful something like that would happen to her. She said she was surprised that it hadn't already happened. Sharon would tell her to fuck off and storm out of the room, puffing away on a cigarette. "You just mark my words," Mom would say. "You're in for a miserable time, the way you live your life, it's not right. You deserve whatever you get. No man will marry you, not after what you've done, you little witch."

Then Mom'd say to me, "Take a bath, honey. You spend too much time with your cousin. Go take a bath." She'd tell me how important it was to keep clean and even though we didn't have much money, we did have soap and water, and there was no excuse for being dirty.

I ran away from home a million times. The police would catch me on the freeway and I'd make up some story about how my mom had forgotten to give me bus

11

fare to school and I had to walk. But they'd take me to the police station, call home and send me back. Nobody ever asked me why I left. My mom would tell me, first thing through the door, "Take a bath. Walking on the freeway like that, what in the world's got into you?" Sometimes I would make it to my cousin's house and spend a week or two with her, but it wasn't the place for me. Finally, I got sent to juvie, juvenile hall, then to foster homes, and finally, a live-in center. I didn't go back home for years. I used to get home visits, but no sooner than I'd get home, I'd leave and stay the night with Sharon. She was the only one who knew what had happened to us, she shared my world, she made me laugh.

When I was sixteen I was sent back home and the first place I went was her house. My mom lived in Pacific Beach and Sharon lived a couple of blocks away. She never lied to me about what she did. She worked downtown at an exotic massage parlor south of Broadway. A month after I got home, late one night, she came pounding on the window of my room telling me to come outside. "It's three o'clock in the morning, Sharon, what's going on?" "Just get out here." She was crying. I jumped out of bed, got dressed and sneaked out the back door. It was dark and I couldn't see her clearly. "Come here. I can't walk very well, help me to my house, I don't want to be by myself. That son of a bitch, motherfucker!" "Who are you talking about?" Then I noticed the blood on the front of her skirt.

"It hurts, goddamn it, it hurts, that son of a bitch!" I put her left arm over my shoulder and I walked her home. She'd make me stop when it hurt too bad, cussing and crying the whole way. "I'm gonna get me a fucking gun and kill that bastard." We got to her apartment. I was scared. I guess I'd always been afraid, in the back of my mind, that something would happen to her, just like Grandpa said. "She drives men crazy," he would say, like she would be responsible for anything that happened. At fault. I lay her down on the bed and ran to get some ice out of the fridge. I don't know why ice, I think I just wanted to get out of the room. I was afraid to look at what had happened. I came back to the bedroom and she was laying on the bed with her skirt and panties off, bleeding all over a towel she had put under her. Then I started to cry. "What's the matter with you? I'm the one that's cut." Then she laughed and asked me to hold her. "You got to go to the hospital, call the police. . . ." She laughed again. "The police, you've got to be kidding. It was a cop who did it." No. I didn't believe that. I couldn't. Grandpas, brothers, police, everyone had to be who they were supposed to be, the order, the role, something to count on. "Hold me. It really hurts." I lay down next to her, and held her like she used to do with me. She put her head on my chest and started crying and telling me how it hurt. She was like a kid and I was the adult. "Look down there and see how bad I'm cut." I wanted to say no, I didn't want to see her bleeding, see her cut, I was afraid. "I need to know how bad it is, I can't see it." I rolled her off of my chest and moved down her body. I opened her legs. I felt like I was going to faint. There was blood trickling down onto the towel. I wanted to cry, but I held it back, I kept it to myself. She was sitting in a pool of her own blood, cut up by some man. The cut was about three-quarter inches and went from the bottom of her vagina halfway around to the back. I started feeling the cut inside of me, it hurt. For an instant, her body was mine. I was cut. Whoever did this, did it to me and to Sharon. "Is it bad?" "Yeah, it's pretty bad. We've got to get you to a doctor or hospital or something." "No way, they'll want to know how it happened. They'll call the cops, no fucking way." "You could bleed to death." She laughed. "I'll be fine. Give me my purse." I walked over to the dresser and got her purse and gave it to her. She told me to get her a glass of water. She took the water and shoved a couple of pills in her mouth and handed it back to me. "Lay next to me till I get to sleep." I moved over to the bed, lay down next to her, put her head on my chest and stroked her head. She talked about being kids, about Grandpa and cousin Mike and about how she was going to get a gun. Next time, nobody—cop or no cop—was going to fuck with her like that, screw her and cut her up and laugh about it. She'd get a gun, stick it to his head. She'd get his ass. She said she hated crying, she didn't like for people to see. "You got to fight, don't let them see you cry. Look them in the eyes and say, 'OK, motherfucker, you mess with me and I'll get your ass.' You hear me?" I said I didn't want to have to fight all the time. "You got a

13

choice?" she said. "Never mind. Anyway you won't have to worry, nothing will happen to you. You're a good girl, a goodie, goodie girl, just like Mary Lou." She laughed and said, "Doesn't really matter, does it?" She fell asleep while I lay there crying.

After that night I didn't go back to my cousin's. A couple of weeks later, I woke up in the middle of the night. I sat straight up in bed. Someone was in my room, sitting on my bed. He had his hand on the inside of my thigh. "You are having a bad dream," he said. He was whispering. "It's just me." His hand securely fixed on my leg, slowly moving down. I wanted to cry. I hated this. "You got to fight, don't let them see you cry. Look 'em in the eyes and tell 'em, 'OK, motherfucker, I'll get your ass.'" I looked him in the eyes, the man who knew no evil, victim of temptation. "You get your fucking hand off my leg or I'll scream so loud everybody in the house will wake up." "You are having a bad dream," he said. "Bullshit, you get your hand off of me or I'll yell." He smiled. "No one will believe you." "Try me," I said. He looked at me. What the hell is she doing, talking back. "You're gonna turn out just like your cousin. And here I thought you were such a good girl." "Fuck you. Get out of here." He looked at me, "You little witch, dirty little witch." I raised my voice, "I said get out of here now." He pulled his hand off my thigh, the skin felt bare, exposed, like right after being shaved. "Be quiet, I'm going." He went to leave, he turned around and looked at me as he hit the door, "Evil little witch." I yelled, "Leave." He was out the door. I lay back down in the bed and I thought, "I'll get your ass." Sharon was right. I moved out of my mom's house. I worked at the Navy Hospital in the evenings and on weekends while I finished high school. I was going to be the first in my family to go to college. I was going to do something with my life. I was going to forget.

Nobody knew my family, what had happened to me. It was my own life now. I had a boyfriend, an apartment, a job in a hospital. Navy Hospital is right next to Balboa Park, facing onto Pepper Grove. On Saturday I would walk through the

14

park instead of taking the bus. Pepper Grove was a place we used to go to as kids. It had a playground with swings and picnic tables. It was familiar. I knew this place. I'd walk through it daydreaming. One Saturday, I was walking through the park, I didn't notice anything. I didn't see them coming up from behind. I just saw the swings and the picnic tables. "Hey, look here. What's your name?" I turned around and saw two guys walking behind me. I didn't say anything, I looked around and didn't see anyone else. I picked up my pace and walked faster.

"What's the hurry? What's your name?" I didn't turn around. I didn't want to see them. I thought, what the fuck do they think they are doing? They yelled at me again and I looked at them over my shoulder. Then out of nowhere came a third guy, standing right in front of me. He grabbed at my chest, "Must be at least a 36C. Big tits. You know what women are good for, huh?" He laughed and so did the other guys. "Huh, you know? Fuckin 'em and sucking their tits, that's what they're good for."

15

I tried to get around them. I yelled. One of them spit on me. The other pulled my head back by the hair. I started yelling, the third one stuffed something in my mouth. I freaked. They punched me and pulled me toward the edge of the hill and down into the canyon. I kicked one of them, "You fucking little witch, you kicked me, bitch." He hit me while another one ripped at my skirt.

I thought I was going to pass out. I couldn't breathe with the rag in my mouth and I couldn't get my hands free. They were kicking me and I thought I would choke. Like Mary Lou. It went through my head, like Mary Lou. I fought, I think I did, I don't know. I don't remember if I did anything. I just remember them yelling at me. "Dirty little witch. Fucking bitch scratched me." I passed out. There was a hand on me, I was soaking wet from sweating and I was gasping and the old man looked scared. "You alright, I saw some boys running from here as I came over the hill. Then I saw you." I didn't know if I should believe him. I thought, he might be one of them. He was a man, old like Grandpa.

I didn't know if it was over. I started to cry. I tried to get up, my back and legs ached. "It's alright. Can you get up? What did they do?" I didn't know. I didn't know what happened after I passed out. Maybe they thought they had killed me and got scared. I got home somehow. I walked into the apartment. And I could hear my mom's voice in my head. "Take a bath honey, you're dirty. You need a bath, dear." "Evil little witch."

I call on my own, on the silenced, on the betrayed, on the other, the executed. The cheated, the slaughtered, raped, murdered and torn open. "Give me your strength. Give me your counsel, your rage and your will to come at last into the light" (Marge Piercy).

Something happened to me. Something here in this town I grew up in, on the streets that I walked and where cousin Sharon worked. I walked into the back door to find it. A new lesson. Challenging the past. A resistance to division, driving a stake in Grandpa's crotch. My best friend Sylvia and I were at college, surrounded by people outraged at the war. Brothers and uncles, friends being killed. My oldest brother dead, my second oldest crazy from it. Nothing academic about it. A war far away, in a country I didn't even know existed till my brother Donnie wrote me. Students being shot, black, brown and white, because they wouldn't shut up. A meeting was called, Sylvia and I wanted to do something. It was a women's meeting against the war. I walked in and sat down. Sylvia couldn't make it; her dad had wrecked the car after drinking a quart of whiskey. I listened. My brother's letter in my head. "This is screwed up, Sis, it's crazy here. I'll go crazy here." I stood up and said, "Me and this chick I know want to do something, we wrote a play about it, we want to help stop this thing. We want to speak up." The women in the room turned around and looked at me like my mom used to. "Take a bath, honey." Then one of them said, "We don't use the word chick." We, I guess, meant all of them. Did it matter so much? More important

16

than the war? "Sorry, didn't mean it, just a word." That made it worse. "Just a word?" There were more wars being fought than I knew. Another woman, with long dark hair, smiled at me. The rest of them sat back. "What kind of play is it?," she said. "Well, it's not actually a play, it's like a scene about the war. Makes fun of the television news, talks about how we're being lied to." She smiled again, "Sounds great. There's a rally next Saturday, can you do it then?" "Yeah, yeah, we can." Her name was Sheri. A feminist, a socialist. It was like having Sharon back, guiding me through the terrain, protecting me, teaching me. We did the rally. The other women in the meeting loved it. Sylvia and I were OK. I became a part of the war. The new war. A woman's war. The final conflict. And it tore me open! Ignited me like a house on fire! Now I understood that "we" meant Barbara, Betty, Beverly, Beth, Cathy, Carol, Cindy, Diane, Donna, Tara, Patricia, Marsha, Djuna, Linda, Deborah, Trina, Michele, Jo Ann, Jodell, Terry, Sophia, Nancy, Maggie, Melissa, Juliana, Volah, Rosemarie, Rhonda, Anna, Sally, Cheri, Janet, Denise, Margaret, Lynn, Susie, Liz, Jane Doe. That thing in between my legs became mine, became magic, clean, accessible territory only to me. I even forgave my mother. Temporarily, she became a sister in struggle. An ally. Stories of women, fighting, challenging, bitches and witches incarnate. Positive, powerful, pissed off. I selected the image. Some would nurture, knit, talk about earth mother, moon sign, eggs and ovum. But not me! I was a regiment commander. A woman warrior, Amazonia, Califia, Sojourner Truth, Madame Binh. I was the commandress of the "kick butt" brigade. We mustered our troops. I made a list. Personal. Grandpa at the top, he died in '64 of TB, but at the top of the list, nonetheless. "You are having a bad dream," he'd say for the last time. I'd kick open the coffin and shoot him anyway, dead or not. Then dad, the cop who cut Sharon, J. Edgar, Richard Nixon, Hyde, Helms, Agnew. Their time was up. My uterus would no longer be a state park, a breeding ground for their workers, soldiers, consumers. My lover would stay at home, he'd bake the bread and clean the barracks, happy to be relieved of combat duty. He was tired of the battle. We'd drive through the streets in big trucks, brooms in hand, demanding that all women send out the woman-bashers, every man that won't take no for an

17

answer, hiding on your couches, drinking beer, and watching Monday night football! Out on the sidewalk, I'd stare them up and down, point my broom at their crotches and yell, "Menstruate or die!" Shivering in their boots they'd start to bleed, cramping up and miraculously, in that moment, realize the suffering of women, demand equality for all, and recant the death of every witch, bitch, queer, burned at the stake of white, male, heterosexual, State power. Now we were called strident, aggressive, dykes, real bad girls, separated off from the nice ones, women gone mad. Telling everything we knew. We were sisters in struggle, no blueprint for movement. Making history everyday. We were alive. I called Sharon to enlist her in the ranks, she laughed and said no thanks, she worked nights and needed to get her rest. "Just don't forget me," she said. "Don't forget who we are. Don't judge." "Never," I said. "You were the first sister." Grandpa's attempt to divide us, a miserable failure. "Women drive men crazy." Not true. Men drive women into the ground, boot heel marks digging into their necks. I did battle everyday, my class showing in every meeting. Differences arose and we turned in on each other, making mistakes, hurting each other, wounding. Ten years of battle, never getting close enough to the enemy, spending too much time looking for it in ourselves. It did us in. But the seed was planted. I knew history, I helped make it. Being burned at the stake of in-fighting would never remove that knowledge. No longer about good and evil, but right and wrong, just and unjust, power and abuse. We had been connected, bridges built, gaps filled in. We were a part of something human and enduring and indestructible. Maybe we had done it wrong. "Style is so important in a world of image," Gloria Steinem would remind us. We did do something. Still, combat fatigue set in. I wanted to leave this place, this sunny, beachy, perfect place. It was like family. Everything apparently fine, normal, healthy, vital, fit for a photograph. No questions asked. "Shut up." "Don't rock the boat." "What you see is what it is."

Before I left, I called Sharon. She'd been promoted, working at La Costa Country Club. She told me she'd gone down on Robert Goulet and that he dyes his hair and comes too fast. I told her I was leaving, didn't know when I would be back.

18

She said she would miss me. I asked her why she never left. She said, "The weather, this is the only city in the country where you can give head on the street 365 days of the year. You'll be back," she said.

She was right. But by the time I came back home to this place, four years later, Sharon was in prison. She had been living in a house that had a methamphetamine lab. A feeling of disconnection, fragmentation, nonresistance, hit me. Old battle scars prevented the brigade from banning together. Just as before, I started over. I had a boyfriend, an apartment, a job, at a hospital even, University Hospital this time, not Navy. Every event on the TV news now became a private matter. I missed the nightly discussions about what they were getting away with. Idealism was out of fashion. People had done their time. The enemy would prevail. The few hearty ones continued, working, organizing, believing. Feminism was seen as a necessary step in a period of development, obsolete, brought under the auspices of institutions, respectable, occasionally belligerent, but integrated. And I was susceptible. Secretly, I would pull out my Marge Piercy poetry and remind myself: "Despair is the worst betrayal, the coldest seduction." My lover, a liberal humanist, was patient with my frenzied outbursts of anger. "They're getting away with murder, taking everything back." But now the real crime seemed to be identifying them; old dogmatism, give it up. The past was still lodged in me and I longed for the battle to be well-defined again. I tried to find a way to submerge the knowledge, the passion, the sense of movement. Ten years ago I would have gone to prison to visit Sharon, to reclaim her. Brave and loud, knowing the injustice, believing. But now, the idea of seeing her trapped, locked up, put away, seemed too much. Age of Ice. I filed away information, saved it in a place where it wouldn't infect the whole being, the being that had a daughter, a family, a job, a presence in their world. It was like being in drag, with the occasional slip of the tongue. Self-help, self-esteem, self-fulfillment, self-aggrandizement, self-pursuit. Not all bad, I guess, but too singularly focused. I would whisper to myself out of fear of being overheard, "We are all still part of each other."

19

"You are having a bad dream." I lay in front of the television. I didn't move. The news was on. I didn't care. "Did you see that?" Menthol smoke filled the room, again? "Did you see that?" "What?" I remember saying, a long time ago. "She's dead." "What?" The TV noises sounded like they were miles away. A young woman being interviewed on TV, charging the police with using her, fucking her, befriending her. Bad girl. She looked like such a kid. The interviewer playing it up with all the vibrato he could muster, El Cajon Blvd., street walking. Shots of women, mini-skirted, smoking cigarettes, waiting for a trick. The division, the sorting out, just like Grandpa. These were those kinds of girls. "They make men do things, drive men crazy."

"She's dead." "What?" "She's dead. They found her . . ." "Tijuana riverbed," I remember. But not this one, not this time. She was found on Sunrise Highway, nude, with gravel in her mouth. A warning: snitches die. Good girls never tell. No big searches, no woman manhunt, no images of a family crying, but still, sweet-faced and disappeared. Sharon had said, "They raped her and strangled her, and stuffed blue rags down her throat. You know the kind of blue paper rags they wash your windshield with at the gas station." No, I thought, not this time. "Nude, with gravel in her throat." Unsolved. Not Mary Lou, Donna Marie this time. And soon to follow, too many more.

"You are having a bad dream." File it away. Names like Speck, Di Salvo, Bianchi, Jack the Ripper. Romantic heroes, imitated and loved. Grandpa. "I wonder if Grandpa did it? What d'you think?" I told her to shutup, I didn't want to talk about it; and, no, I didn't think Grandpa did it. "Yeah, you're right, lots of people could have done it." I remembered now. No longer eleven years old, I believed it, Grandpas, brothers, police, it could be anyone. With every successive death I thought how glad I was that Sharon was in prison. The next few years forty-three more women are found. Files stamped NHI, No Humans Involved. Police are demoted, then promoted. Nothing to do, nothing to do with me. "You're a goodie, goodie girl." She laughed, "Doesn't matter, does it?" Bad girls, some with police

20

contacts, transients, drug users, some with no names. "Don't forget who you are." Sharon would say, reading between the lines again. The earth spitting up the remains of women "dumped." The less valuable. "You are having a bad dream." Using the divisions, the sorting out, the good and bad as reasons for somebody getting away with murder. And I remembered what a friend said years ago: "Somebody's getting away with murder and they're still out there." This time it's not just about Mary Lou, but now Donna Marie, Cindy, now so many more. Each woman murdered, a face, a daughter, a cousin, a human, a woman. The invisible regiment re-forms itself. It was inevitable. We will do something. "Good girls never tell" was his lie, not mine. Old friends, new ones, resisting, filling in gaps. Talking with knowledge. "A woman's life is a human life," we would say and it makes sense all over again. They had taken back too much. "We'll give these women faces, names, mothers, fathers, make them human. Post up the faces, let the world know. For the ones we can't find we'll ask our friends, stand-in for a woman, give her a face." And we did. Armed with the ancient knowledge this time that every face is our face, every slaughter a crime, and the belief that resistance, out of fashion, is inevitable. I look at them, the photos, the faces, and study each line, nose, mouth and eye, as if it were my own, your own. Because to those who murder us, we are all the same.

21

In memory of:

Jane Doe #1, age unknown; Donna Marie Gentile, age 22; Tara Mia Simpson, age 18; Patricia Smith, age 31; Marsha Shirlene Funderburk, age 25; Djuna Demetris Thomas, age 20; Linda Joyce Nelson, age 27; Linda Kay Freeby, age 30; Deborah Ann Stanford, age 24; Trina Carpenter, age 22; Jane Doe #2, age unknown; Cynthia Maine, age 26; Michele Riccio, age 19; JoAnn Sweets, age 36; Jodell Jenkins, age 28; Carol Jane Gushrowski, age 20; Theresa Marie Brewer, age 26; Jane Doe #3, age unknown; Sophia Glover, age 37; Nancy Allison White, age 22; Jane Doe #4, age unknown; Cindy Jones, age 25; Kun Yueh Yeh Hou, age 41; Melissa Gene White, age 22; Juliana A. Santillano, age 25; Volah Jane Wright, age 37; Rosemarie Ritter, age 29; Rhonda Lynn Hollis, age 21; Anna L. Varela, age 32; Sally Ann Moorman Field, age 19; Sara Finland Thornton (also known as Gedalecia), age 36; Diana Gayle Moffitt, age 24; Jane Doe #5, age unknown; Cheri Lee Galbreath, age 25; Melissa Sandoval (also known as Adrianne Flores), age 20; Janet Moore, age 27; Sandra Cwik, age 43; Mary Wells, age 31; Diana Ampura Luna, age unknown; Cynthia Lou McVey, age 26; Linda Christine Marler, age 26; Danise Marie Galloway, age 33; Jean Nicolette Frye, age 22; Margaret Orosco Jackson, age 46; Felix Abarca, age 24.

Because to those who murder us, we are all the same.

22

WOMEN'S WORK PROGRAM, LIZ CLAIBORNE, INC.

Through its Women's Work Program, Liz Claiborne, Inc. commissioned contemporary visual artists to create these images which were displayed on nearly 200 billboards and transit shelters throughout the Bay Area in 1992 to raise awareness of the growing epidemic of family violence in America:

Margaret Crane/Jon Winet, Courtesy Liz Claiborne, Inc.
Barbara Kruger, Courtesy Liz Claiborne, Inc.
Susan Meiselas, Courtesy Liz Claiborne, Inc.
Diane Tani, Courtesy Liz Claiborne, Inc.
Carrie Mae Weems, Courtesy Liz Claiborne, Inc.

23

Concurrently, Liz Claiborne, Inc. provided funding for a new, centralized, 24-hour crisis hotline in the community and spearheaded the formation of a volunteer community group dedicated to raising funds and providing on-going assistance to the San Francisco Domestic Violence Consortium. As a result of these efforts, the Consortium has received $388,500 in new funds to date, and a new level of awareness about the issue continues to grow.

Margaret Crane/Jon Winet, Courtesy Liz Claiborne, Inc.

Margaret Crane/Jon Winet, Courtesy Liz Claiborne, Inc.

Barbara Kruger, Courtesy Liz Claiborne, Inc.

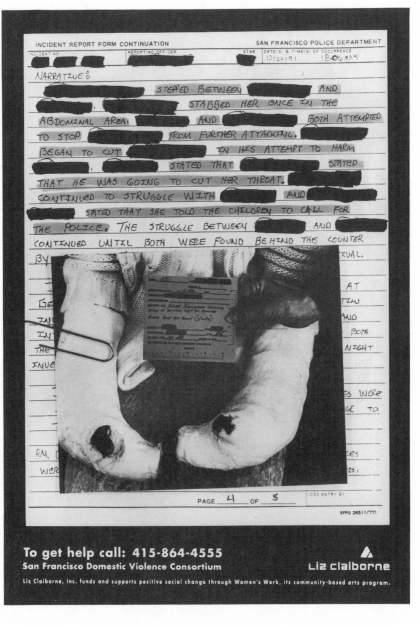

Susan Meiselas, Courtesy Liz Claiborne, Inc.

91%의 학대를 당한 여성들은
자녀들이 그들이 맞는 것을
보았다고 합니다.

63%의 학대를 하는 사람들은
그들의 어머니가 학대를 받는 것을 보았거나
자식으로써 학대를 당했습니다.

그들은 보고
듣고
배우고
그리고 반복합니다.

폭력의 무리를 막읍시다.
(415)864-4555 로 전화를 주십시요.

리즈 클레이본 주식회사(Liz Claiborne, Inc.)은 공동체의 순환 재정 프
로그램인 여성활동(Women's Work)을 통해 긍정적인 사회적 변화에
기금과 후원을 합니다.

Liz claiborne

Diane Tani, Courtesy Liz Claiborne, Inc.

91% of abused women say that their children have seen their beatings.

63% of all abusers have seen their mothers abused or were abused as children.

They Look, Listen, Learn, and Repeat.

Stop the cycle of violence.

To get help call: 415-864-4555
San Francisco Domestic Violence Consortium

Liz claiborne

Liz Claiborne, Inc. funds and supports positive social change through Women's Work, its community-based arts program.

Diane Tani, Courtesy Liz Claiborne, Inc.

"I'd rather my man should hit me, than for him to jump-up and quit me."

Is a joke girl-friend

To get help call: 415-864-4555 San Francisco Domestic Violence Consortium

Carrie Mae Weems, Courtesy Liz Claiborne, Inc.

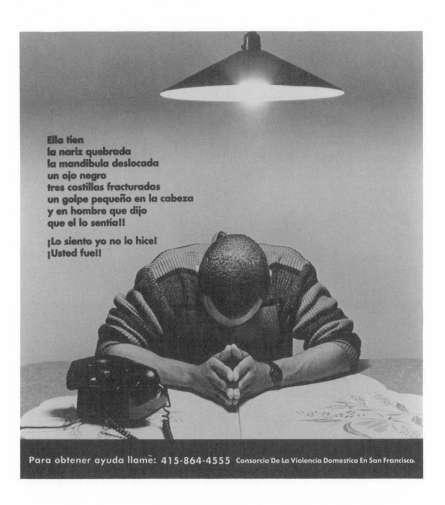

Ella tien
la nariz quebrada
la mandíbula deslocada
un ojo negro
tres costillas fracturadas
un golpe pequeño en la cabeza
y en hombre que dijo
que el lo sentía!!

¡Lo siento yo no lo hice!
¡Usted fue!!

Para obtener ayuda llamé: 415-864-4555 Consorcio De La Violencia Domestica En San Francisco.

Carrie Mae Weems, Courtesy Liz Claiborne, Inc.

She had:
a broken nose
a displaced jaw
one black eye
three fractured ribs
a mild concussion
and a man who said
he was *sorry!!*

But sorry
didn't do it!
You did!!

To get help call: 415-864-4555 San Francisco Domestic Violence Consortium

Carrie Mae Weems, Courtesy Liz Claiborne, Inc.

ON CURATING FEMINISM, ACTIVISM & ART

Laura Brün

The forums in *Critical Condition* are excerpted from a Fall, 1992 conference on Feminism, Activism & Art organized in San Francisco by two community-based arts organizations, The LAB and SF Camerawork. We decided to produce the conference as a response to the recent focus on women's issues in America resulting from media spectacles such as the Clarence Thomas Supreme Court hearings at which Anita Hill testified, the William Kennedy Smith trial for rape charges brought by Patricia Bowman, and other events that provoked the wrath of women across America, sparked a national debate about violence against women, and caused the media to proclaim the resurgence of feminism in America.

In the media-produced election "Year of the Woman," women watched the changing of the guard with a kind of morbid fascination. We watched Thelma and Louise kill a rapist and drive to oblivion. And grimly noted the hysterical reaction of the American male to this blatant display of female "power." We watched the demonization of Anita Hill and Hillary Rodham Clinton as women "out of control," and marveled at the ease with which this characterization was justified and accepted. We watched female politicians wearing skirts and tightly controlled hairdos, toning down their messages, and defending their ability to lead in office against an onslaught of gender-based criticism, especially in regard to fiscal matters where women are traditionally considered to be "loose," like prodigal slot machines in Las Vegas. We watched the media sensationalize and profit by "true stories" of battered, raped, and angry women in a proliferation of made-for-television movies cashing in on female rage.

Aware of the fact that the glare of the media spotlight would soon be focused elsewhere, we wanted to organize a conference that would bring attention to the range and depth of the work of feminist activists and artists in the last decade. Over sixty women—visual artists, writers, performance artists

33

and activists—presented their work, discussed the politics of their work in panel discussions, and spoke with audience members who challenged, supported and elaborated on the speakers' perspectives.

What emerged was the barely contained fury under the surface of the American female psyche during the Reagan/Bush era. The conference demonstrated that feminism was alive and well over the last twelve years: it had just gone underground. That, in fact, it thrived in a counterculture of lesbian and heterosexual women activists who worked to defend what precious little ground was gained in the 70s by maintaining battered women's shelters; fighting censorship, apathy and fear; learning and teaching women's history, feminist theory and practice; making art about all these things; and writing for our lives.

These forums in *Critical Condition* document a particular time and place, and also the many years of hard work by feminist artists and activists in America, the full extent of which we have only begun to recognize. The discussions instruct us to examine history—personal and cultural—to reclaim a sense of purpose. And that to do so, we must reopen wounds that have never quite healed, share and acknowledge our experience of violence, and continue to form new alliances, information networks, and support systems for each other in years to come.

34

Rupert Jenkins

I began curating *Murder as Phenomena*, an art exhibition that coincided with the Feminism, Activism & Art conference, after coming across several disconnected photo projects about killers and killings. Interestingly, two of the three projects concerned women murderers, one of whom stood out as an icon from my childhood in the1960s in England—Myra Hindley, the so-called "Moors Murderer."

Hindley, like Aileen Wuornos thirty years later, was reviled in the British press as a pitiless and monstrous aberration. Aileen Wuornos had just been arrested for the murder of seven men in Florida when I began my project. Her case was instantly sensationalized by the tabloid media, yet the thirty years since Hindley's arrest had added an unfamiliar element to the media circus— Hollywood and the instant made-for-TV movie. (Wuornos claims that even before her arrest the police were negotiating with her lover over the movie rights to her story.) Wuornos became a *cause célèbre* for just about everyone, and fore- shadowed many of the issues addressed by the artists in the exhibition and the Feminism, Activism & Art conference: domestic abuse, judicial prejudice, capital punishment, serial killing, media sensationalism, and women's right to defend themselves.

As I gathered works from across the country, the breadth of interpretations of what constitutes murder—nuclear war, weapons research, animal abuse, police brutality, to name a few—astonished me. I chose, however, to focus the exhibition on individual acts and the consequences of those acts, and to allow the exhibition catalog to extend that context to include political and ideological interpretations. Tellingly, I received a huge proportion of work from women artists, and a long tradition of work by women about violence, particularly violence against women and children, was revealed to me.

For instance, a series of public performances had been produced by Suzanne Lacy and Leslie Labowitz in December, 1977, in response to the media's handling of the Los Angeles "Hillside Strangler" killings. For the exhibit I chose four images by Marin Karras that document one public event: *In Mourning and in*

35

Rage, a performance ritual that was carried out on the steps of the Los Angeles City Hall in front of City councilors, activists, the public, and the media. A motorcade deposited nine mourners—seven-foot tall veiled women—outside the steps of City Hall. They were joined by one woman clothed in scarlet, and a ritual began in which each of the nine mourners stepped forward and stated "I am here for the ten women who have been raped and strangled between October 18 and November 29." A chorus echoed her: "In memory of our sisters, fight back!", and the mourner was wrapped in a red scarf by the woman in red, who declared at the end of the ritual, "I am here for the *rage* of all women. I am here for women fighting back!" *In Mourning and in Rage* received extensive media coverage, and prompted the emergency listing of rape hotlines, as well as the redistribution of money to self-defense workshops for women and city employees in Los Angeles.

The legacies of *In Mourning and in Rage,* which showed how artists can play an active role in the politics of social change, can be found in the San Diego *NHI* project fifteen years later by Deborah Small, Elizabeth Sisco, Carla Kirkwood, Scott Kessler, and Louis Hock. The project was successful in raising public awareness and open debate about the deaths, although somewhat ironically some of the projects' media coverage has come from shows like "Inside Edition," the type of program implicitly involved in the sensationalism of similar violent crime.

Susan McWhinney, Cathy Greenblatt, and Leslie Ernst (New York/San Francisco/Laguna Beach) constructed an interactive, computer-based timeline of women murderers that was devised to confront notions that women killers are a contemporary phenomenon evolving out of the feminist movement. *(Ain't) Natural History* revised history to advance the concept of a woman's natural right to be aggressive, and indicted the juducial system's gender-bias against women in cases as far apart as Ruth Ellis (1925), Alice Crimmins (1956), Amy Fisher (1992), and Aileen Wuornos. A hypercard database of women murderers was accompanied by a printed timeline dating back to the seventeenth century that emphasized "the points at which history repeats itself, as do certain types of crimes, the methods by which those crimes are committed, and the judicial, social, and media responses to those crimes."

Theory Girls (San Francisco's Laura Brün and Jennie Currie) also took the case of "lesbian serial-killer" Wuornos to investigate the anti-feminist backlash against women. In their interactive piece the viewer, faced by a mural-sized image of Wournos handcuffed on the witness stand, listens to a telephone conversation between two women discussing Wuornos and the failures and successes of feminism in relation to violence and women. In the gallery installation, as one stood listening to the conversation, the viewer was faced on one side by a huge grid of portraits of the forty-five murdered women in San Diego County, and on the other by a series of color photographs of death chambers, taken throughout the US by Lucinda Devlin. The portrait of Wournos, looming above the telephone, served as a visual metaphor for her current existence, caught between her earlier life of survival as a prostitute working the Florida highways and her current life of incarceration on death row.

Janet Dodson (San Francisco) spent months meeting and talking with convicted women in California's Frontera prison. Her project is crucial to understanding the perspectives of women whose only recourse was to kill to save themselves from further abuse. Battered Women's Syndrome—a complex set of symptoms similar to post-traumatic stress among combat veterans—helps explain why a woman can stay with her abuser, often to the point of dying at his hands. But when a woman turns around and kills her batterer she faces a gender-biased court system that often responds with savagely harsh sentences. *Prison Project I* consisted of photo documentation of a clemency hearing at the California Institution for Women-Frontera, together with personal testaments four women wrote to Dodson, who displayed them with their family snapshots and other texts.

37

As is often the case with broad projects like this, *Murder as Phenomena* raised more questions for me than it answered. The show, in varying contexts, addressed mass-media influences on our perceptions of violence. Our complicity in condoning and accepting violence is clearly influenced by the media—that ubiquitous dog-chasing-its-tail—although no one will ever agree to what degree. Television, once invented to sell us the American Dream, now sells us the American Nightmare. Our society is confused—it believes that whatever behavior is acceptable on television is acceptable in real life, an understanding constantly reinforced by media projections of life as being "just like a movie." Yet as we descend toward economic paradigms wherein funds for education are balanced against funds for jails, it comes as no surprise to find artists striving to probe the truth of our societal psychosis. Their insistence that we not turn away from bitter truths is crucial to our healing, lest a memory killing breeze drag us into a vortex of acquiescence and chaos.

AILEEN WUORNOS

"AMERICA'S 1ST FEMALE SERIAL KILLER"

FORUM I: WOMEN WHO KILL

Elizabeth Sisco
Susan McWhinney
Leslie Ernst
Janet Dodson
Jeanne Finley

Women who kill are usually the most sought-after "criminals" on the streets. Defying the myth of female passivity, they are viewed in today's cultural landscape as more dangerous and aggressive than any man committing a comparable crime. Through studies and interviews, the artists and activists here talk about who is actually behind bars, what crimes they did commit, and the price they are paying for defending themselves against their own disappearance. For example, 90% of the women on death row are lesbians, so what does this tell us about the justice system? And the value of the life of a woman who transgresses dominant family values in this country?

Amy Scholder

Elizabeth Sisco

NHI—No Humans Involved, one of an ongoing series of public art projects about community issues addressed the sexual assault and murder of forty-five women in San Diego from 1985 to 1992. The project began on February 19, 1992, with the unveiling of two billboards bearing the picture of Donna Gentile and the letters NHI. Gentile was the second victim in the string of murders. A sex worker and police informant, Gentile was found strangled to death, her mouth stuffed with gravel, a month after she testified against two police officers.

Two days after the billboards went up, we opened a rented storefront gallery in downtown San Diego to display portraits representing the forty-five murdered women and distribute a book that described in detail police involvement with Gentile and a number of the other dead women, and police mishandling of the murder investigations.

Carla Kirkwood's performance, MWI—Many Women Involved, ran for three nights in the gallery space. A community forum addressing the series of murders and violence against women was held in the gallery space on International Women's Day. The goal of the project was to pay tribute to the murdered women, raise public awareness about the series of murders and the botched police investigation, and relate the local reaction to the crimes to larger social attitudes towards gender violence.

The series of killings became referred to routinely as the "prostitute murders." By labeling the series this way, San Diego law enforcement skillfully manipulated public perception in order to hinder awareness and outrage, and to cover up the extent of police involvement with a number of the murdered women. Since we are conditioned to believe that violence and death are known occupational hazards for sex workers, we respond to their demise with apathy or a resigned willingness to blame the victim, to accept the murder of a prostitute as one of life's harsh realities. At the same time, we are relieved that such brutality could never be visited upon those of us who comply with societal mores.

Our attempt to break through the stereotyping that characterized this depiction of the murdered women was partially undermined by law enforcement's response to the project. On the day the billboards went up, in one of his rare public responses to the project, Richard Lewis, head of the task force assigned to investigate the murders, told reporters: "NHI is an old term that goes way back in murder history, back to the old days on the East Coast." Lewis fictionalized the term, stating he first heard it "when I was a young kid reading detective magazines." He also said police officers did not use the term in reference to the murders under investigation by the task force. Lewis' spin on the meaning of NHI was quickly adopted by electronic and print media alike. Ninety percent of the stories about the project referred to NHI as "an old time police term," i.e., a bit of folksy nostalgia without contemporary currency.

Lewis' claim that officers don't use NHI is refuted by published accounts of police officers who admit to using the term. In 1990, the *Sacramento Bee* quoted a San Diego police officer: "These were misdemeanor murders, biker women and hookers . . . we'd call them NHI's—no humans involved." While the exhibit was open, a police officer and a paramedic both wrote comments in the gallery book acknowledging ongoing use of NHI. Calling himself an investigator of misdemeanor murders, the police officer said he had been trained to disregard the humanity of victims from the "darker side" of life.

The media coverage of the project perpetuated the myth that all the slain women were prostitutes, drug addicts, and transients. Again, the overwhelming majority of TV news and print stories routinely referred to *NHI— No Humans Involved* as a project about the "prostitute murders" although we repeatedly emphasized the diversity of the victims—beauticians, waitresses, homemakers, a word processor, nurse, stock supervisor, grocery clerk, hospital kitchen aid, and a writer. Less than half the slain women were known sex workers. However, public perception of the murders was framed by this generalized labeling of all of the victims as "bad girls."

While the media was sympathetic to the concept of presenting a human face to the murdered women, coverage of the project tacitly reinforced

43

what Linda McCabe, a legal advocate, has called a "nationwide pattern of denial." McCabe states, "If we can find some fault with the victim's behavior or demeanor, then we can rest assured that we are invulnerable to such attacks."

Because of the specter of police involvement with a number of the murdered women, San Diego officials—from the mayor to the district attorney to the police chief—did little to refute the idea that these forty-five women deserved to die because of how they lived.

This message can be contrasted to that surrounding another series of murders that took place in San Diego in 1990. In this case, all of the victims were brutally sexually assaulted and murdered by an intruder who entered bedrooms in a quiet, middle- class neighborhood, and killed five women. The largest manhunt in San Diego Police Force history stopped him. Police held daily press briefings from a special command post set up in the neighborhood and a city councilman went door-to-door warning residents to take extra precautions. The press and police emphasized that one of the women was a college student who worked at a sporting goods store. They de-emphasized the fact that she also worked part-time as a nude dancer. Nude dancing was not an occupation that fit this particular victim profile.

When asked by a reporter to compare the speedy resolution of the murder of Cara Knott, a college coed found strangled in San Diego in 1986, to the foot-dragging occurring in the growing "prostitute murder series," a sheriff responded, "It's hard to evoke as much empathy for a prostitute as there is for a pretty little college coed."

Selective law enforcement reinforces social double standards and promotes a belief that bad girls get what they ask for. But the lines separating "good girls" from "bad girls" is mutable and any one of us could appear to be a "bad girl" at any time. Nancy Allison White, the twentieth victim in the San Diego "prostitute murder series," was a stock clerk from Santa Ana, California, whose car broke down at night along the I-8 corridor where a number of the murdered women's bodies were dumped. According to Detective Tom Streed, the initial lead investigator in the cases, "White's clothing was not inconsistent with what would

44

arouse a person involved in the other cases." White's casual summer attire of shorts and a tank top on the evening of her murder placed her in jeopardy. Detective Streed's dangerous appraisal of Nancy Allison White's demeanor is representative of the insensitivity exhibited by law enforcement in their investigation of these forty-five murders. It is also indicative of a larger social reflex to blame the victim. This attitude increases the danger every woman faces when out alone for any reason.

The purpose of *NHI—No Humans Involved* was to humanize the victims and demonstrate that violence against any woman is unacceptable. The gallery exhibition literally lent a face to the forty-five murdered women. From 1985, when the killing began, until 1992, images of only seven of the women appeared in the local press. The police refused to release photographs of the others on the grounds that their publication might hinder the investigation. When we were unable to obtain photographs of all of the actual murdered women, we asked women from the community to act as stand-ins for thirty-seven of the women for whom we could not get images. The stand-ins were educators, homemakers, administrators, therapists, social workers, writers, artists, lawyers, scientists, ranchers and entrepreneurs. The use of stand-ins provided a message of solidarity with the murdered women and all women in the community. It was a public acknowledgment that violence against one woman is a threat to all women, and that to brand victims of violent sexual assault as prostitutes, drug addicts and transients stifles genuine public concern and gives a false sense of assurance to other women.

45

The *NHI* project created a moment of public awareness and a broader sense of community in San Diego. It gave a voice to Pat Riccio, mother of one of the slain women. Pat spoke with great courage and eloquence about the neglect, disrespect, and callousness of the authorities investigating the death of her daughter. The project provided a place for the family of Linda Christine Marler to join together to remember their lost sister. Speaking about the series of murders within a public art context allowed San Diegans to examine seriously the issue of violence against women. People were genuinely astonished to learn of the magnitude of the series of murders and the depth of police involvement with the crimes. Through the project we were able to assert that no woman deserves to die the brutal death these women suffered: "The punishment for prostitution is not execution" (Linda Barker-Lawrence, National Victim's Center, Dallas, quoted in the *San Diego Union*, February, 12, 1989).

However, somebody is still getting away with murder. The task force created to investigate the murders has disbanded. There is an attempt to pin multiple murders on men who had been in jail for a number of years at the time the murders were continuing. Law enforcement successfully used the stigma against prostitutes to cover up their own corruption. Sadly, the police are a reflection of the society they serve. Hopefully, *NHI—No Humans Involved* shed light on the danger faced by all women in a society that denies the true culprits in the "wages of sin," favoring the comfort of the false dichotomy created by the good girl/bad girl label.

46

Susan McWhinney

Petite Treason: Crimes against the Matriarchy

> "The story of women who kill is the story of women."
>
> —Ann Jones, *Women Who Kill*

Just as history has obscured many of the accomplishments of women, from the arts to the sciences, it has also obscured crimes committed by women. The biggest omission of all being the fact that women murder and do so much more frequently than most of us know. To quote Enid Bagnold, "A murderess is only an ordinary woman in a temper." It isn't hard for me to believe this is true, since I can relate to a woman who goes into "a temper." Women do kill. And their motives can usually be attributed to a very specific set of circumstances, underlying which are American principles of economics and property ownership, firmly legitimated by media coverage. It would be far more useful to examine this fact than to continue to perceive and portray the act of murder by women as an unnatural and isolated event.

Out of my interest in this subject came my involvement in a collaborative work with Leslie Ernst and Cathy Greenblatt. *(Ain't) Natural History* takes the form of a timeline charting the course of the American Murderess. It is a partial framing of the lives of women who kill, or are believed to have killed, in relation to the political, judicial, and social climates of their times. The premise of the piece is twofold: first, to say that women have murdered throughout history; and second, to show that women in America appear to have a very specific orientation to murder. Motivations may loop and repeat as social, political, and judicial landscapes do, but the basic issue is almost always one of survival.

The relationships of women and men to murder are worlds apart. While men often kill for pleasure, retaliation, or "honor," women, in this country, murder mainly as a means of survival. Legal definitions of murder and motive, from serial killing to self-defense, are predicated on the methods and motivations by which men kill. When applied to women, these definitions and laws serve mainly to obscure relevant issues. As politics and morals have made a rapid, frightening swing to the Right, murders committed by women have come to the media forefront. Current media coverage reflects the fears of a society trying to control its women. Women's cases are moralized and sensationalized in a way that characterizes few cases involving male killers. The notable exceptions are those in which the male perpetrators fall into the category of Other: Jeffrey Dahmer, John Wayne Gayce or Ted Bundy—the "homos" and "porn freaks." Joe-average-white-heterosexual is very rarely covered by the media to any degree, if and when he is caught. Straight white boys with a penchant for brutally murdering women seem to be low on the totem pole when it comes to catching bad guys.

Some interesting cases and their attendant media coverage that are relevant to this discussion are as follows: In a recent California murder case, a husband and wife are charged in the murder of five transients in order to cover up a cattle rustling scheme. The coverage on this case places the emphasis on the "elderly female" who committed five gruesome murders. It was not until the end of the article that it was noted her husband had played an equal role.

Amy Fisher, the "Long Island Lolita," goes to jail for five to fifteen years for the attempted murder of her lover's wife. Fisher was a seventeen-year-old high school student at the time of the shooting. Joey Buttafucco, the thirty-seven-year-old business man, who allegedly set her up as a prostitute and encouraged her to shoot his wife, was never looked at seriously in conjunction with the actual murder attempt. He was recently indicted on charges of statutory rape only after several witnesses came forward to testify that Buttafucco had bragged about having sex with Fisher.

A lesbian couple who conceived a child through artificial insemination was recently found guilty in the abuse and subsequent murder of the child. Legislation was proposed to ban lesbians from being artificially inseminated. No such legislation is proposed for straight couples who maim and murder their children.

49

Aileen Wuornos is arrested and given the death sentence for the murders of five men. Wuornos called it self-defense. A prostitute who worked in desolate areas, she was attacked, raped, and abused by her johns. The State says she is a serial killer. This charge is implausible, given that the definition of a serial killer is one who kills for the specific purpose of sexual arousal within a specific power balance. Women are not usually dominant in this power dynamic, and Wuornos certainly was not. She was arrested, tried, and convicted within a year of the first murder.

Two things are interesting to note here. The first is that after Wuornos' trial, several people came forward to claim that some of the "victims" had in fact been known to have abused their wives and girlfriends. Apparently, the violent abuse from which Wuornos claims to have been defending herself was entirely in keeping with the personalities of the men she killed. The second is that while Wuornos' capture and conviction were both quickly executed and highly publicized, the murders of several dozen women in the San Diego area have gone not only unsolved, but have also been almost entirely ignored by the media.

The differences in these cases speak volumes in relation to the history and roots of public and judicial response to female committed murders. The female victims in the San Diego cases, referred to by the police as NHI (No Humans Involved), would be more aptly named NMP—No Man's Property. These cases are not given the high priority as that of Amy Fisher, who shot at the "property of a man" (female-to-male murder used to be tried as Petite Treason, roughly, a crime against the patriarchy), or Aileen Wuornos, who shot at men. In the case of the lesbian couple, the issue seems to have been replacement of a male in the traditional role of father and this, rather than the murder, was the crime for which the couple was on trial.

Victim is a word frequently used in conjunction with females. I use the word victim with hesitancy and more to bring up a point. The use of the word victim presupposes helplessness and innocence. In relation to violent crimes, it connotes a certain form of physical powerlessness. It is important to understand that in this country the majority of murders committed by women are motivated by the woman's need to survive, and that within this framework women kill in many ways and for many reasons. For some, they are provoked by extreme physical and emotional violence committed upon them by someone they are dependent on. For others, it is an attempt to survive economically in a culture that often socially and economically cripples women under the guise of protecting them. While a woman killing an abuser in self-defense is eons away from the woman strategically plotting out murders for economic gain, she is, at the same time, not so distantly removed. Both murders are committed as acts of survival. In one sense, the woman who kills is taking a step away from victimization through the act of eliminating her abuser or remedying her financial situation. Unfortunately, she is all too often pulled back into the role of victim as soon as a judicial system designed for men and a media machine geared towards sensationalism get hold of her.

51

(AIN'T)
NATURAL HISTORY

What are little boys made of, made of?
What are little boys made of?
    Frogs and snails
    And puppy-dogs' tails,
That's what little boys are made of.

What are little girls made of, made of?
"Now the weapon of death descended ten
What are little girls made of?
times, once with sufficient force to slice
    Sugar and spice
through her father's cheekbone, sever an
    And all things nice,
eye completely in half and continue on its
That's what little girls are made of.
path deep into his skull."

What are young men made of, made of?
What are young men made of?
    Sighs and leers
    And crocodile tears,
That's what young men are made of.

What are young wemen made of, made of?
"...one of them notticed a buzzard picking at
What are young women made of?
something. The birds meal turned out to be
    Ribbons and laces
the hand of a badly decomposed corpse
    And sweet pretty faces,
hidden beneath a piece of carpet."
That's what young women are made of.

COPS: WE GOT FIRST FEMALE SERIAL KILLER

Man-hater used sex to lure seven victims, shocked police charge

AMERICA'S first female serial killer is a man-hating lesbian who posed as a prostitute to lure at least seven men into her web of death, a police investigation reveals.

Aileen Carol Wournos, 34, a hatchet-faced blonde with stringy hair and a heart-shaped tattoo on one arm, has been charged with first-degree murder for the killing spree.

Her victims were found lying beside roads in rural areas of central Florida and southern Georgia.

Some of the men were nude or only partially clothed, and condoms were found at the scene of some of the crimes.

Most of the men had been robbed, but chief investigator Steve Binegar, of the Marion County Sheriff's Department, told The GLOBE: "Wournos is a killer who robs, not a robber who kills.

"She worked as a prostitute just to lead the men to their deaths," the investigator adds. "Her motive for the killings was her hatred of men."

As The GLOBE reported in our Jan. 8 issue, Wournos and her lesbian lover, Tyria Moore, 28, became the subject of a massive manhunt after they were spotted near the scene of one of the killings.

Moore has not been charged in any of the kill-

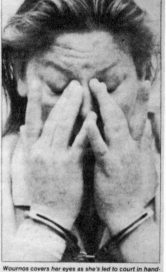

Wournos covers her eyes as she's led to court in handcuffs. She's a lesbian who despises men, police say

Suspect Aileen Carol Wournos, 34, bears a striking resemblance to the sketch police used in their manhunt

ings and is expected to be a key witness against Wournos, police say.

Wournos was alone when she was arrested in a seedy bar in Harbor Oaks, Fla. "She was not armed and she surrendered quietly," says sheriff's office spokeswoman Della Cormier.

"She and Moore had known each other for six years and had a lesbian relationship that later, according to them, developed into more of a 'sister' relationship."

Wournos was a leap-year baby, born Feb. 29,

Five of the unlucky victims: From left, Douglas Giddens, Gino Antonio, David Spears, Troy Burress and Charles Humphreys. At least two others suffered brutal deaths

1956, in Michigan. She spent the past 20 years as a drifter in Florida and other Southern states.

She worked occasionally as a hotel maid or a prostitute whenever she needed money, police say.

One investigator believes that her demeaning experiences as a hooker instilled in her a bitter hatred toward all men.

In 1981, Wournos was jailed for armed robbery and she was arrested again in 1986 for carrying a concealed weapon.

People in Harbor Oaks knew Wournos and Moore as tough, hard-drinking women who hung out at rough bars. Wournos was also spotted buying "extra-strength" condoms at a local convenience store.

"I always thought they might be troublemakers," says Rose McNeill, owner of the Fairview Motel. "They stayed here for about

two months. One night, a man and a woman got into a screaming argument in another room. The next day, Carol said to me: 'All men are evil — Satan.' "

The two women spent a

She boasted about pushing guys around

lot of time drinking at the Fly Inn, a bar across the street from the motel. "Carol told us her name was Lee, and she'd spend hours drinking beer and shots of whiskey," says owner Penny Miles.

"She used to boast about boyfriends and how she pushed them around. A number of customers complained about her obnoxious behavior and we

had to tell her never to come back."

Wournos was also a regular at a biker bar called The Squeeze Inn and The Last Resort Inn, where she was arrested.

The Last Resort has vulgar T-shirts and bras nailed to the ceiling. The manager, a 280-lb. man named Cannonball, says: "Ty disappeared a couple of weeks ago, but Wournos was almost living here. She'd sleep outside on a seat from a pickup truck under a lean-to."

Another bar patron, who refused to give her name, says Wournos confessed to her several weeks before she was arrested.

"I was really spooked," the patron says. "Carol boasted to me about killing men she met. She scared me and I tried to stay away from her. She was always drunk."

— GEORGE HUNTER

Wournos & her lover lived at the Fairview Motel. "I thought they might be trouble," says owner Rose McNeill

Leslie Ernst

I wanted to start out today with the image of the black widow, and talk about how this image has been used to portray Aileen Wuornos and her case.

Aileen Wuornos, a lesbian who worked the Florida highways as a prostitute to support herself from the time she was a teenager, was arrested on concealed weapons charges and later charged in the murders of five middle-aged white men in northern Florida. Her arrest in January, 1991, came as US bombs rained down relentlessly on Baghdad. Consequently, her case initially received very little national coverage, like most domestic events at that time. Aileen Wuornos was convicted in the state of Florida, and in view of her case and what it represents, she stands to be the first woman executed in the state since 1840.

Questions around violence, questions around power, questions around the distinction between victim and perpetrator all come up in her case. I want to show a clip from an interview with Aileen Wuornos in prison, which aired on NBC's "Dateline" at the end of August, 1992. She has now been convicted on five counts of murder, after having pleaded no contest to subsequent charges. Wuornos has claimed self-defense in all of the killings, stating that while she was working as a prostitute, when men refused to pay and then assaulted her, she responded in order to survive.

In this clip of the interview from Florida's death row, the visual framing of Wuornos is so tight that she is not "contained" within the picture, in contrast to the well-composed commentator, Michele Gillen.

MICHELE GILLEN: You're explaining now that these men were abusive, in your opinion. You understand, now, that for many people, because you were a prostitute, they don't understand how a prostitute can be raped.

AILEEN WUORNOS: I don't understand how nobody can understand how a prostitute can be raped. Because when a man rapes a woman, he assaults your whole body. He puts his . . . (censored by the network) . . . down your throat, cramming it down

your throat. He tears your hair out of your head. He beats your face in. He—he
rips your . . . (censored by network) . . . wide open.

Aileen Wuornos' case effectively disrupts the assumptions held in the
question, "Didn't she ask for it?" Her actions and her life—including a history of
incest and violence in her family—bring many of the issues raised by this
conference to a head. Wuornos' claim of self-defense in the murders of middle-
aged men in northern Florida registers the most direct challenge: Wuornos said,
"I'm supposed to die because I'm a prostitute? No, I don't think so."

The tabloid, the *Globe*, branded her as "a man-hating lesbian who
posed as a prostitute to lure at least seven men into her web of death." Aileen
Wuornos, as a working prostitute, has been depicted as an ultimate femme fatale,
a black widow. Crediting the media in the apprehension of Wuornos and her lover
Tyria Moore, Sergeant Bruce Munster of the county sheriff's office in Marion,
Florida stated: "It was very important that we warn people that these very
dangerous women were out there. Hitchhikers, women who seemed to be
stranded on the roadside. They could be killers. And we wanted to warn people
about that."

55

Initially postponed due to controversial film deals which took place
prior to her arraignment, her case was railroaded once it did get to court. In
court, the prosecuting attorney, John Tanner, was particularly vindictive.
Regarding her initial confession, he stated that she never once mentioned self-
defense in that original statement, when in fact, she talks explicitly about self-
defense and explicitly about the assaults more than fifty times in her initial
confession. In addition, whereas Wuornos was on trial for the murder of Richard
Mallory in 1989, Tanner introduced mention of charges in four other cases. The
jury deliberated for only an hour and a half before they arrived at the death
sentence.

The social value of a woman's life is starkly revealed in the level of
the investigation applied to serial murders of women (often alleged prostitutes)
as compared to that of middle-class, middle-aged, white males. In December

1989, the body of Richard Mallory was discovered, and the investigation which followed culminated in the arrest of Aileen Wuornos one year later. By contrast, consider, for instance, the Green River murders in the Northwest which began in 1982—reports vary, but the number of women who have disappeared is estimated at upwards of one hundred. In *The Age of Sex Crime,* Jane Caputi cites the Seattle official's description of the projected profile of the Green River killer: "We're looking for an intelligent person, a person that might have animosity against women in some way or perhaps has a biblical interpretation toward cleansing women such as baptizing them in the river or whatever." By far the largest serial murder in U.S. history, public awareness was slow to evolve in the case, as the estimated one hundred missing are young women of color, and female prostitutes.

After nearly a decade, these murders remain largely unsolved. And it is important to note that several links have been made to police involvement in the killings in Seattle and Los Angeles (including evidence that the first Green River victims were killed using choke holds in which police are trained). Similar incidents have been reported on the East Coast; I think it's very plausible that Aileen Wuornos was fighting her own disappearance.

In the collaborative effort (*Ain't*) *Natural History* at SF Camerawork, Susan McWhinney, Cathy Greenblatt and I came together to work collectively to articulate a history of which Aileen Wuornos is a part but not an exception. Although Wuornos has been dubbed "America's First Female Serial Killer," the label is typically used to describe violent homicides committed against women by male perpetrators. Applying this title to Wuornos denies a history of women who have responded to the violence in their lives with rage, defiance, and violence. Our approach is not to condone or condemn behavior but to complicate rather than essentialize issues of violence and notions of transgression, to get at the specific conditions and motivations of women who have killed. In exhuming this history, we've found that there are many cases in which women have committed murder multiple times, often as a means of survival.

I'm interested in examining this lineage of women's transgressions,

56

as well as the distinct responses that women are taking on in the '90s. Wuornos is a woman who definitely said no—not only did she not ask for it, she wasn't going to take it.

Janet Dodson

During the summer of 1991, I was watching a Donahue show about children who had killed abusive parents. I thought, this is a subject that I would like to explore. Here are children who struck back against an abuser. To which category will they be assigned by society? In victim/oppressor terminology, what, if either, will they be considered? I prefer to think of them as activists in the most primal sense. They struck back solely at the ones who had abused them, instead of taking their rage out on innocent people.

This interest led me to the Hall of Justice in San Francisco in early September of 1991. I had planned to research the names of children and women who had been convicted of killing abusive parents or spouses. I quickly found out that you get nowhere without a specific name, a specific year of conviction, and a specific jurisdiction. However, Victim's Assistance was able to give me the name of a woman who told me that there would be a clemency hearing on September 17 for women who had killed abusive spouses. I called Assemblywoman Jackie Spiere's office for details. Spiere's assistant informed me that the hearing was closed, but that they would arrange access for me to go to the hearings.

Prison Project I is a project documenting research conducted at the first major hearing in the state of California, held on September 17, 1991, at the California Institute for Women-Frontera, to investigate the Battered Women's Syndrome, how such evidence may be admitted into a court of law, and whether or not eight women who killed abusive husbands would be eligible for clemency. The eight women whose cases have been under consideration for clemency were the prisoners with whom I met, and with whom I established an initial written correspondence.

The focus of *Prison Project I* was to provide a forum for the convicted women to tell their own stories, as opposed to having a third person represent their lives through an interview structure. In our written correspondence, I expressed to them my desire to create an art piece that would be composed of a

58

family photograph taken at the time the abuse was occurring in their lives, and a statement about their lives at the time the photograph was taken. I was interested in the idea of the family photograph. Do members of families really look "normal," or are there clues to dysfunction, perhaps hidden in the eyes or body language? I thought that presenting these photographs along with the "true" story—the statements written about family life during the period that these photographs were taken—might provide some important clues.

The response was not immediate. I must have written at least thirty letters before three women agreed to the project. Two of the eight women whose cases were being considered for clemency, Brenda Aris and Christy Camp, were very enthusiastic by the time they agreed to participate. I also agreed to open the project to all members of a support group formed at the California Institute for Women called Convicted Women Against Abuse. As a result, one of the women in the group, Lori Bartz (who was not convicted on murder charges) expressed her desire to participate in the project.

I was puzzled that only three women were interested in sharing their histories with others, considering (what I later discovered) the very public attention that all of them received from television media. When I returned home the night of the hearing, I turned on the television. The program "20/20" was airing a special on these same women. I have since seen them featured on "Inside Edition," the local channel 7 evening news, the "Home Show," and as a feature story in the San Francisco Examiner. I thought, well, I suppose I don't really fill a need for these women to tell their stories when, as it is, they receive so much coverage. However, one of the women who chose to participate in my project told me that a lot of the prisoners only had one photograph of their abuser, and they weren't willing to risk losing it. That photograph of the man who had so violently abused them was one of the most precious possessions in the world to these women. As it turned out, two of the three women who make up Prison Project I gave me photographs which did not include the abusive spouse.

Christy Camp sent me three pictures. In fact, she was the only one

59

who sent me a picture which includes her now-deceased husband. Lori Bartz sent me a photograph of herself alone (taken in prison). Brenda Aris' photograph was of her and her three children, taken by a professional photographer after her husband's death. In her statement she wrote, "During this time [of the abuse], I often found myself looking at our photo album. I was always the one who took the photographs, so all the pictures were of Rick and the kids. I used to look at the pictures and think, 'After I'm dead, they won't even know what I look like. They won't even have a picture of me.'"

Brenda believed her husband would someday kill her. At the hearing on September 17, Brenda related the following while being questioned by Assemblywoman Spiere:

BRENDA: I've had my jaw broke, my ribs cracked, several bruises.
SPIERE: You never called the police, though.
BRENDA: Never.
SPIERE: And why is that?
BRENDA: Because you don't call police on him. You're considered a rat if you call the police. He was brought up in juvenile hall. You know, you just don't call the police. You know it would be worse. He already told me, you don't ever call the police on me 'cause I will kill you. I knew you just don't call the police. I mean, I knew that.
SPIERE: So on the evening of the death, there was a party that someone was having, and you were both planning on being there.
BRENDA: Yeah, we were there, and uh, one thing, he was upset. He was upset because I couldn't get the money to get him some drugs. I always had to come up with the money, and if I didn't it was my ass. So, I always tried to make sure he had his drugs. What happened was, I was talking to a friend, and he had called me over and he was upset, 'cause you still haven't got me anything, and I said no. So he backhanded me and knocked me down and told me to go to my room. I didn't go to the room 'cause I didn't want to cause a scene. I didn't want everyone to see me. My girlfriend was there and said, do you want me to take the children? So I said, well,

61

take Chris, the oldest one, 'cause I knew I was getting my ass beat that night. You know when you're getting your ass beat. You know and so then I said, yeah, will you take Chris 'cause I don't want her to be here. I don't want her to see this. The other two were sleeping. They were fine so she took her and I went back to the bedroom. Well, I was there for a while and I was ready for bed. He then proceeded to come into the room and started screaming and yelling and slapping me—got on top of me and was hitting me—pulled my hair so hard I thought my neck was going to break. He just kept punching me wherever he could and he was hitting me and he told me, I've had it with you. I don't think I'm going to let you live till the morning. I've had it, and I knew when he said this to me—I mean, I just knew he meant it. I wasn't gonna live.

A key part of a battered woman's defense resides in the admission into evidence of the testimony of an expert witness. A leading expert witness is Lenore Walker, a psychologist who began testifying in court in 1977. Testimony such as hers was necessary to help juries understand the psychological state of women who had been battered and had killed their spouses. Juries needed to know what role the Battered Women's Syndrome had in such cases. In fact, Walker mentions the Brenda Aris case in her book, *Terrifying Love: Why Battered Women Kill and How Society Responds*. Brenda shot and killed her husband, Rick, while he was passed out, fearful he'd resume beating her and actually kill her when he regained consciousness. The result of the judicial limitation imposed regarding the nature of the admitted expert witness testimony was that Brenda Aris, who was so battered by her husband that at the time of her arrest she was covered from head to toe with black-and-blue marks, was found guilty of second-degree murder. Without an expert witness to validate a self-defense claim, or a voluntary manslaughter plea, Brenda had no chance in court.

Most of the convicted women were refused any testimony by an expert witness. Part of the purpose of the September 17 hearing was to request that Battered Woman's Syndrome be admissible testimony in these sorts of trials.

One reason that it is necessary is that, as Gloria Allred stated: "We need to understand the concept of safe places—the concept of how women are socialized into subordination dependence, and then also the thought that they should be independent somehow and get out." She proposed that the courts recognize that the concept of a reasonable woman's standard should be applied—not the concept of what a reasonable man would do and whether he would think he was in fear or danger. For instance, a reasonable man's defense is, "If you punch me in the face, I have the right to hit you back." In other words, supposedly a man can kill you right there on the spot in self-defense. But, obviously, men and women are not physically capable of the same actions. Many battered women have to wait until the man is passed out or asleep to kill him, before he wakes up and finishes beating her for good.

One other point that bears mentioning regards the question, "Why didn't you just leave?" Seventy-five percent of the women killed by batterers are killed after having left or while trying to leave the batterer. Walker states in her earlier book, *The Battered Woman:*

63

> The batterer truly believes that he will never again hurt the woman he loves, and that he will be able to control himself from now on. However, he also believes that he has taught his partner such a lesson that she will never again "behave" in a way that tempts him to physically assault her.

And, it seems, that the batterer is not the only one who believes the woman will learn her lesson. As Susan Faludi states in *Backlash:*

> In 1985, some psychoanalysts at the American Psychiatric Association decided it was time for masochism to make a comeback as a "new" disorder in the professional *Diagnostic and Statistical Manual of Mental Disorders,* or *DSM,* the bible

of American psychiatry. . . . Worst of all, the diagnosis
threatened to invite a return to treating battered women as
masochists who court domestic violence. The APA panel
included these traits in its definition of the new masochists:
"choosing" people who "disappoint" or "mistreat" them and
remaining "in relationships in which others exploit, abuse, or
take advantage." The panel illustrated these traits with an
example of . . . a spouse who criticizes a mate, thus
"provoking an angry counter-attack."

Pop psychology states this idea differently. Faludi reminds us that in
the late '80s, codependency became *the* addiction or disease:

The professional medical journals supported this illness
metaphor, deigning codependency as "a disease of
relationships" in which the individual "selects a life partner
who is chemically dependent or who is otherwise dysfunctional." (The individual they had in mind was almost always a
woman; the codependency was even defined in female
terms—its original model, the alcoholic's wife.)

And finally, to put all this information into historical perspective, in
her book, *Women Who Kill*, Ann Jones describes the historical shifts in cultural
understanding of why most women kill, and explores their subsequent treatment
at the hands of the court. During periods when women were more vocal in
demanding their rights, those who killed men were punished more severely than
they might have been during relatively "tamer" times. In fact, throughout history
a fairly stable number of women kill, accounting for about ten to fifteen percent
of all homicides. An analysis of the homicide statistics kept by the Centers for
Disease Control (CDC) indicates that, for the first time since the CDC began to

65

keep this data, "In the period 1979-1981 there was a decrease in the number of women killing men, but an increase in the number of men killing women; yet the numbers of women being sentenced to prison keeps rising."

Women who kill men serve twice as long as men who kill women. It is still a crime against patriarchy to kill an abusive husband. And I do mean patriarchy, because, in fact, the government had no interest in these abused women other than the kind of example that would be set if wives struck back against their husbands.

67

Jeanne Finley

I'm going to play an audio tape from a series of interviews I did at the Carson City Women's Prison. Here's a little background about how I had the opportunity to meet these women and how these discussions that we had came about: I didn't go to the prison to speak about violence or aggression. Rather, I was working on a film about home and the individual's relationship to home, the construction of one's memory of home when one's home has been lost or taken away. But, what emerged was that it was impossible to speak about home or domesticity without speaking about violence.

I had been invited to the Women's Prison to give a presentation and since I was doing a piece about home I thought it would be interesting to talk to these women about how they construct home within the prison. During my presentation I selected some works, one of which is called "Beyond the Times Foreseen," and it deals a little with domestic violence. After I'd given them a sense of the nature of my work, I set up appointments with anyone who wanted to come talk with me. I spent three days talking with the women there.

I was assigned an assistant, Mickey. She was a very quiet, twenty-two-year-old girl who had been in prison for six years. She absolutely refused to be interviewed, and that was fine. But she was with me as I talked for several days with the other women. She had walked out of my slide presentation because she was disturbed by the domestic violence that was dealt with in "Beyond the Times Foreseen." Finally, she said, "I'm really sick of you asking all these questions. I want to interview you." That was great. She put me in front of the camera and did a lengthy interview, and then after I'd answered all her questions, she said, "I *do* want you to interview me now. I'm going to set up the camera. . . . You're asking all the wrong questions. You're skirting around all the issues." Because I wasn't asking about their crimes; I was asking them about home. She said, "In my case, you're going to have to be much more direct." So, she asked everyone to leave the room, and we began a very long series of talks that continued over the period of a year of my going back to talk with her as well as two other women, Barbara and Sandy, to whom I'd gotten fairly close, as close as one can under those circumstances.

Mickey was convicted of a double life sentence. Her defense could have been shaped around the defense that Janet Dodson spoke of, which is the fact of abuse. But she refused to testify publicly about the abuse that she suffered in her home. There are lots of reasons for that. And no one really knows the truth about the crime she committed. Even after all the time I spent with her, I have no idea about many aspects of her crime. I know she was involved in planning the murder of her mother and that her boyfriend probably did do the actual murder itself with machetes and hacksaws, weapons of that nature. I do know that it's something about these relationships around domesticity, between one's place of refuge and one's memory, and among all of those things we look to as safety, and about how all that is so inextricably connected to violence. That's what this piece is about.

The idea of victimization is something these women are very consciously trying to turn around in their lives. Through education and their experiences in prison with the other women, they have been able to redefine their identities, from a position as victim to one of empowerment. Although they detested prison, they were very grateful for the idea of home that they constructed in prison—grateful not for being incarcerated, but for the relationships with the other women that they established. That is something I'm very interested in personally. I know women have been victimized, but it is absolutely essential that we stop defining ourselves as victims. These women have done that for themselves and are, therefore, an inspiration to me.

69

AUDIO TAPE: NOMADS AT THE 25 DOOR

MICKEY: I do think of this as my home. I don't think of the institution as my home. I think of it as my home because of the people that I've come to know here.

I learned about restraints during sexual action, before age seven, when I was younger, but I don't remember when it first happened. I learned the famous catch-all phrase S/M when I was eight. I learned about that in detail, heavy detail.

BARBARA: In my home it was, uh, I was more or less the mom. My sister and brother called me Mom for years, and when I was fifteen, her third marriage, I decided I was just sick of dads. My second father sexually abused me.

SANDY: We're not a very close family at all. When I was three years old, I was molested by my father, and when I was nine, I was molested by my brother. And it was denied in my family that it had happened.

MICKEY: When I was sixteen, I met up with this guy. Coming from the type of family I came from, it really fascinated me that somebody would take an interest in me. During a meeting that he and I had, I had showed up and I had bruises around my neck. And he saw me one time where I had twenty-four stitches in the side of my face. And he . . . I think it kind of built up, and ultimately, one very long day and night he took matters into his own hands.

SANDY: I married. I think I was about sixteen when I married and had three children right off the bat. I stayed in my marriage for ten years and was an addict and was an abused wife for that time. So I hooked up with this man, another man that controlled me, uh, that I allowed to control me, I think. And we went to Las Vegas and I committed a crime there. And several months after that I was arrested and sent to prison with a sentence of five to life.

BARBARA: I got married at sixteen, had a son at seventeen. At nineteen, my son was abducted from me. I was beaten, left for dead. I was told by psychiatrists and psychologists that I had a death wish, but that I didn't have that guts to kill myself, which was real right on, because, you know, I found drugs. Now I'm thirty-two. I have five convictions. I thank God that I'm alive because I know that by all rights, I shouldn't be. I've OD'd numerous times. I've been shot at. Guns have jammed when people have fired them at me. I've been in numerous situations where I should be dead. Drunk behind the wheel, things like that. I know that it's only a power greater than me that keeps me alive.

MICKEY: Like I said in the beginning, I am here for life, two lives, uh . . . for murder in the first degree. The ultimate story is that he—I'm here because he killed my mother. He slaughtered her basically, the way I put it. And I am the one that found her. I was being kept in an apartment, and when I finally got a chance to get out of there, and I headed home, I knew I was going home to something, but I didn't know what. I had no idea that I was going home to that. I mean, I look at it like something out of *Friday the 13th.*

SANDY: I have no contact with my family at all now. But I have a family. In here. I have people in here that I love and care about, a lot. And I never realized that I would have to come to prison to find acceptance. And it's real tragic that a person has to come to prison to find that they're OK. Of course, the things that I did that brought me here are not OK. And not long ago I got a letter from my oldest daughter, and she wrote in it about how much she missed not having a mom and about how it hurts her because all of her friends have moms. And when they do things at school or other activities, that her friends' moms are there.

MICKEY: And without somebody there that you are intimate with, it's very empty. I think that a lot of us here depend on that. We look to that, and we also look to it because we see it as hopefully being something different from the way we had it on the streets. I mean, women find that when they turn around and get into a relationship *in prison,* that, hey, this is nothing like my boyfriend out there. I think the good relationships that I've had were extremely painful when they ended because they didn't end because they broke up. They ended because their time ended in this prison. It's painful to have to sit back and watch them walk out the door and make a life for themselves. You're happy for them, don't get me wrong, you're so happy they finally get that chance! But I'll never forget how it felt to have them leave. The people and the friends that I have here, that I've come to know, are kind of like the family I've never thought of having but got, and hey, it's neat.

BARBARA: When I first came here, whoa, I got into a lot of trouble. I was . . . they took the needle out of my arm and threw me in prison. But a lot of the old convicts took me under their wing. They saw I was having problems, girls that had been here a long time. And now I have somebody I call Mom. She's been here eleven years. I have somebody I call Brother. I have somebody I call Sister. And it's really sad that you have to come here to feel that kind of love. I was a trustee and I got hurt at a community job and I fell into boiling water and chemicals and I was in the hospital for eleven days and I came back and I couldn't walk. And these women here literally washed me, washed my hair, fed me, dressed me, took care of me like maybe nobody else ever did. And I'm leaving in August and it's, you know, a little ways off, but some of my friends have life. And I know once I walk outside that, we call it "25 door," "freedom door," a lot of them I won't ever see them again. And I wrote a poem, 'cause I do poetry a lot in here, it helps me . . . deal. The name of it is "How Do I Leave My Sisters?"

How do I leave my sisters?
who held me in the night
that nursed me when I was sick
and loved me with all their might.

How do I leave my sisters who
helped me through my strife
I have to . . . I really have to . . .
cause some are doing life.
How can I leave these cons?

who mean the world to me
How can I leave behind these
friendships, in order to be free?

When no mail came for me
they were there to comfort
with welcome sympathy
At Christmas, alone and lost,
They were my family.

Now I've paid my dues
now I can be free
but I've got to leave them
I'm beggin' on my knees—
God don't forget them,
for I cannot
Cause without 'em I'd never have gotten this shot
to walk out 25 door
to the real world again
because I couldn't of done it
without my convict friends.

73

MICKEY: About going home, I feel that a lot of people in here are so lucky. They have kids, they have parents, they have a family, they get to go home! Maybe not to the same exact home that they left, but they get to go home. And I wonder, what is that like? You know, and the first thing that runs through my mind sitting here is, like, they get to go home to their mothers. Right on, and then it's like, I can't, she's not there anymore.

Yolanda López
Wanda Coleman

74

Angela Davis writes in Women,
Culture and Politics, "The very same social
conditions that spawn racist violence . . .
encourage sexual violence." The misogynist
criminalizations, murders and sexual abuse
we're discussing at this conference are related to
all crimes against marginalized "others." They
spring from the same encrusted system of
oppression. Yet, at the same time, specific
hysterias that ignite hate crimes are
excruciatingly individual to each group singled
out for attack. So that, the fatal shooting of
African-American teenager Latasha Harlins can
be linked to the murders exposed in the NHI
project.

As the ACT UP slogan warns,
Silence = Death. Access to the media, to the
channels that distribute information throughout

society, is essential to survival. Yolanda López and
Wanda Coleman discuss the enormous chasm between
their lived experiences in the world and representations
of people of color in popular culture and mass media.
They expose the danger of living in a society where the
real relationships to power are distorted and denied in
the media-fueled myth of American life. And in their
work, they challenge myriad lies and manipulations
that keep dominant culture powerful.

In America, two parallel universes exist.
Here, women are creating dialogues about their daily
lives, their cultural identities, achievements, sexualities,
and their most intimate experiences with power,
violence, and abuse. The other universe is the glossy
world of mass-produced culture, of television, movies,
popular press. There, the real issues of women's lives
are often trivialized and falsified, dolled up and given
the spin that sells. Political issues are obscured, and
economic reality, bleached away.

75

Margaret Crane

Yolanda López

Visibility has been a hotly debated issue among Mexican-Americans, at least since the civil rights movement in the '60s, because much of our history has not been written down, rendering us invisible. However, at the beginning of the twentieth century, a romanticism of life in California, which was tied to its Mexican and Spanish past, did exist.

The derogatory term "greaser" also came into common use at that time. By the 1920s, the motion picture industry was producing a series of "greaser movies," which were so debased in their depiction of Mexicans that the Mexican government protested. (Dolores del Rio, who appeared in many of these silent films, returned to Mexico highly criticized, but was eventually forgiven and became a film star in Mexico.)

Also at that time—the first twenty or thirty years of the century—a lot of cowboy stories about the romantic West were written. This was when Zoro was invented by Johnston McCully in a book called *The Curse of Capistrano,* and O. Henry wrote a short story about a character called the Cisco Kid, which in the '50s was a popular television series.

Women were depicted throughout this time as either romantic *señoritas,* chaste and very beautiful, or as tarts, prostitutes, and women of the street. It's very interesting that this period early in the century also coincided with the great migration of Mexicans because of the Mexican Revolution. There has always been this ambivalence about Mexicans, whether we're seen in the contemporary sense as people who are dirty, liars, and lazy, or we're seen in the romantic sense, as Spanish *señoritas* in old missions. And this ambivalence is still operable today.

In the last ten years, there has been a disconcerting turn in popular culture regarding the Southwestern look. It came at the point when there was the most hysteria about illegals coming across the Mexican border, specifically between California and Mexico. In the late '80s, new immigration legislation was passed so that now if you employ a person without papers, you can go to jail and be fined as an employer. This repressive legislation and the hysteria within the general population that illegals are taking everybody's job, are on welfare, don't pay their taxes, etc., coincided with the popularity of chili pepper Christmas lights, silver cactus earrings, salsas (even one labeled "bandito" salsa, which is a very old image of the Mexican male as a criminal)—all designed and sold by non-Mexicans for a white, middle-class buyer. Contemporary Mexicans and Latinos are seen as dangerous or disgusting or fearsome; and, at the same time, there's a romantic overlay, a nostalgic past that is marketable.

As far as images of contemporary Latina women, we exist almost nowhere. Frida Kahlo is seen very favorably, almost mythically; but, of course, she is dead. Luis Valdez, a Chicano director who did *La Bamba* and *Zoot Suit*, is trying to make a film on Frida Kahlo. Many Chicano actors and actresses protested because he had hired an Italian-American actress to play Kahlo. They felt that he should have hired a Latina, which would have been a very important step in producing some sort of a public image for us. Fearing he would change his mind, New Line Cinema, who originally funded the project, pulled out because they didn't believe the film would be profitable without a white actress. And Valdez came out with a statement saying that his filmmaking is not an affirmative action proposition.

Dolores Huerta, it seems to me, deserves as much if not more praise than Frida Kahlo (but you don't see Dolores Huerta earrings or T-shirts or buttons . . .). Here again is that dichotomy of an historical figure who is completely mythologized, and a contemporary person who is either ignored or debased. Dolores Huerta is the chief negotiator for the United Farm Workers. She worked with Cesar Chavez in the '60s, fighting the agriculture business' attempt to keep workers from being unionized and acquiring everything from a fair wage to health benefits and education for migrant children. In San Francisco, Dolores Huerta was picked out in a crowded demonstration and brutally beaten by the police.

77

In the '70s, I was examining images of Mexican-American and Chicana and Latina women in the United States, looking at images done by the Chicano civil rights movement in publications. And the most consistent image I found of a Latina was the Virgin Guadalupe, which is a Mexican version of the Virgin Mary. I found her to be a very beautiful but passive symbol, and still connected with the Roman Catholic Church, which is repressive not only in its sexism but also in its racism. And so I redid a series of the Virgin Guadalupe as myself, my mother, and my grandmother, playing with and critiquing the image as a passive image, while at the same time paying homage to women, older women, and ordinary young women. That was done in 1978, and there's been a recontextualization of that work that has begun to put it within the framework of the goddess movement. That was the last thing in the world I was thinking about. It implies that I was thinking about creating a new goddess when, in fact, as an iconoclast, I was trying to do away with any kind of worshipping of an image.

There are a lot of Chicanas producing extremely exciting art right now. For example, Ester Hernandez, Juana Alicia, Lily Rodriguez, Nao Bustamante, Laura Aguilar, Consuelo Jimenez Underwood. Latinas and Chicanas are beginning to study our own histories by looking at a philosophical past within Aztec and Mayan cultures, beginning to recreate or restructure the pantheon of gods that exist there, but seeing them not so much as literal objects that we worship but rather as metaphors for our people, our situation in the here and now. We are not recreating our culture with altar-making and the Day of the Dead work. We are not coming up traditionalists. We are trying to take forms that are familiar to us, that we feel in our flesh, and make them work for us now in a very contemporary sense, thereby making them our own.

79

Wanda Coleman

I think a lot of what you're talking about is exploitation in the name of ideology. Now, Los Angeles is supposed to be at the cutting edge of image-making, and I think that it is. Our particular brand of madness is exported via satellite around the world. These images are very powerful, and they do have influences. There's nothing more startling than getting off a plane in Amsterdam and seeing "Green Acres" on television, or having aborigines in Australia ask me what kind of a person Angie Dickinson is. These images carry an awful lot of weight to people in other parts of the world. What comes out of Hollywood is who we are to other people on the planet. It's really quite serious, and you have to deal with these images.

Since the Watts riots of August 1965, blacks have been pushed out of the city. Over 75,000 blacks in the past ten years have been pushed out of L.A. And I'm one of the few who have resisted this pressure, this push that I feel to just fucking get me out of the city. So I took root in Hollywood. I've lived there for the past twelve years.

Last year the city was on the verge of boiling over, primarily because of the verdict in the Latasha Harlins case that had just gone down. Latasha Harlins was a fifteen-year-old black girl who went into a mom-and-pop store that was owned by Koreans to buy some orange juice. Have you all seen the videotape of what happened? She got into it with Ja Dou, who happened to be the old lady on the other side of the counter who no-speaka-English, who assumed that the young girl was probably a thief, which is usually the assumption that operates when you're black, the minute you walk into somebody else's place of business, you are automatically a thief. You were born a pickpocket and a purse snatcher. You are automatically a criminal when you are black and you're born in this country. She thought this girl was stealing so she grabbed her gun and shot and killed this fifteen-year-old girl. When the verdict went down in her case, and that woman went free, there was no support from any other community. The feminist community was totally silent. The Latinos were silent. The Asians were silent. The

Jewish-Americans were silent. This was a fifteen-year-old child. (I was the size I am now at fifteen.) She was not a gang member. She was just a fifteen-year-old child in a woman's body who went into a store to buy some orange juice and her life was taken and there was no punishment for it. And all of these other factions of the city were silent. Where were all of our good feminist buddies? *Mi holocaust no es tu holocaust?*

It's not enough to give off the appearance of having a common cause. There has to be some application and there has to be some action, and there has to be the difficult process of follow-through. This has to be exhibited not only by discussing the images in our culture, but by what we do, who we help, how we make a difference. In other words, there is enough lip service.

So if you're serious, let's talk about some practical applications. Let's talk about distribution networks, so once you create these images you can distribute them. You can make your product, but what in the fuck can you do with your product when you can't get it to market, when the trucks won't carry it and the fucking airplanes won't fly it? We have to work out alternatives to the traditional distribution networks in this country, because THOSE WHO CONTROL DISTRIBUTION, as any good Hollywood filmmaker will tell you, CONTROL THE IMAGES. Why are there not the kind of black films, the kind of Chicano films, the kind of Asian films out there that you want to see in these United States? What kind of progress is it when a piece of shit like *Thelma and Louise* is called a feminist film? Are we late? An effective reversal only takes place when there is equal power. Was that movie a demonstration of equal power? The problem for women is our reluctance to have power.

It seems everyone has to comment on the Madonna syndrome, so I'll say this about Madonna and the white-nigger syndrome she represents. What I'm surprised about after watching her exploit all those young black people on film [*Truth or Dare*], is that I didn't hear any outcry. I didn't hear any outcry and I was really surprised about that. That seems to bring home the lesson that when it comes to white women especially, they're still using their bodies to get over, and WHAT IN THE FUCK IS NEW ABOUT *THAT?* They say she's opening up new

81

discussion about sex. Everything she's doing is as old as the hills. It is a dialogue that has been going on and on, you know, "the world's oldest profession," as they call it. What in the fuck is revolutionary about this woman? Showing her tits in public? What happened between the assassination of President Kennedy and the election of Mr. Clinton that made *that* revolutionary? I mean, she can masturbate in public and make millions. I can't even sell my own story in Hollywood to talk about my version of the black experience. It has NO VALUE. IT HAS NO DOLLAR VALUE.

I think the bottom line of what we're talking about is the value of human life. As long as my life has no value, no matter who you are, if you're white and you're at the top, your life has no value. You're going to have to resolve the stinky problems that attend racism in this country. You're going to have to get to the root issues because it spills over. I don't care what issue you want to bring up. Ecology. Drugs. Homelessness. Fifty-five percent of the homeless in this nation are black males. What does that mean? Forty-five percent of violent deaths of white males over the age of sixty-five are by suicide. What does *that* mean? It's time to get down to the bone and talk about the blood issues that face us all.

DISCUSSION

COMMENT: The media's lack of attention to the murder of Latasha Harlins was disgraceful. Likewise, there were two brutal murders recently in Oregon of Hattie Mae Cohen, a black lesbian, and Brian Mock, a gay man. When national media (television news, the daily newspapers, etc.) don't pick up these "items," there's almost no way to get any national momentum in response to these hate crimes. The message is that their lives are completely disposable.

WANDA COLEMAN: Whenever these incidents occur, unless there are photo opportunities, nothing happens. In L.A. the game is at a max, and people across the nation have finally picked up on the sound-bite phenomenon. Right now there is a lot of factionalism. For example, the media is reporting every time there is a conflict or appears to be a conflict between blacks and Latinos. The news people can't get enough of that. But when there was an attempt to have a dialogue between the blacks and Latinos, not only in public forums but in a cassette called "Black and Tan Club," coverage of it was rejected by the *LA Weekly* as not being of any particular value or importance. So, we can't get our product reviewed, and there's no way of getting it out to our public to let them know that there is some sort of constructive dialogue going on.

When I first got wind of the clashes between the blacks and Koreans, the first thing I did was go to the alternative press. They would not listen to me. And I wasn't the only one who went. I know of four writers and artists who went and said, Look, this is happening in our community. You need to talk about it. There needs to be some public discourse. If there had been some public discourse, IT MIGHT HAVE SAVED LATASHA HARLINS' LIFE.

There is a practical side to this question of being in positions of power, for example, behind the camera. I met my first sheik, an Arab sheik in the mid-1980s. He came into the office with his entourage and his limo and there was this shock of recognition. We looked like brother and sister. *You* look like *me* kind of phenomenon. All my images of what an Arab sheik looks like have been shaped by the images I've been fed of what an Arab looks like. I did not know until the past decade that there were Palestinians who look like me. That there were Arabs who look like me, who have hair like mine. That Noriega is *blood*. Racism in politics is not discussed. The extent to which racism determines our politics in the US is glossed over and not challenged by the people that I expect the challenge to come from, the people who are supposed to be politically aware because of their circumstances and the conspiracy of circumstances in this country that have trapped them at the ideological bottom of this society. I feel that if there were more women or more people of color behind those camera lenses, just in terms of practicality, image-making would be different. The best thing that can be said about someone like Spike Lee is that he has gone blow-to-blow, toe-to-toe, to open up some of those images. He's a great casting director. In

83

Spike Lee's case, well, I think we are entitled to our mediocrities. After all, Alfred Hitchcock had the luxury of being able to make a film over two or three times until he got it right. Why shouldn't Spike Lee have the same privilege?

POEMS BY WANDA COLEMAN

OF APES AND MEN

as we posed around the appetizers, drinks snugged to our lips,
in his cozy digs, overlooked by two very thrilling Rembrandts,
our host, the successful scriptwriter, bent our interest with an
amusing account from his early days

the occasion was the making of a Tarzan sequel. the director
had come up with a daring idea: the movie would open with
several minutes of beautiful footage as hundred of apes and
assorted monkeys scaled African bush and swung through trees
in fierce ecstatic freedom. instead of using the standard
canned simian sound track, the director thought it would be
much more authentic to strip in the joyous cries of the actual
beasts

this remarkable scene would be followed by the majestic
appearance of the Great White Ape himself, sweeping
triumphantly across the screen, the conceptual genius of
having the little critters' actual never-before-done endorse-
ment of the white man as king-of-the-jungle gave everyone
hard-ons

85

elaborate preparations were made. a special
sound stage was constructed. the call was put out.
animal trainers and their tamed hirsute trainees,
from far and near, were flown or driven onto the
Hollywood lot and escorted to the sound stage. the
lights dimmed in the impromptu theatre and the
silent footage unreeled, a slowed-motion spectacle
of hundreds of limbs arched in fluid glory, eyes
flashing, teeth ablaze

there was an amazing lengthy silence as the clip
ended and the lights went up. without prompting
the entire room erupted in sudden violence as the
startled trainers were attacked by their charges
who brutally clawed, bit, shat and threw feces

86

*

later, over dinner, he and i began a conversation
on the state of my race

"your people have made a good deal of progress,
haven't they," our host waved his fork with
authority

"on the contrary," i struggled to conceal my
outraged astonishment to hear this presumably
cultured man utter such bigoted banalities, "the
progress you speak of is quite illusory"

"oh?"

and as i launched an impassioned explication his
eyes lost luster. he rose and abruptly left the table
leaving me with my mouth open

SEX AND POLITICS IN FAIRYLAND

rose red from across the tracks does
grow up to be a knockout. bold with big legs
and all the rest of the equipment necessary
to excite a prince

and if she plays her pumpkins right (she will)
she'll become snow white will acquire
all the material things wished upon

the big fine castle. servants of a darker race
the stretch limo. jewels and furs
champagne for a frivolous breakfast of
scrambled eggs and caviar

a smart dame from across the tracks, rose
has an instinct for opportunity—the savvy it
takes to get over. she knows she's got to score
before she's knocked up, starts to pudge out, or
otherwise loses her looks

this may require compromise—dyeing her hair
henna or ash, special hormones or cosmetic surgeries
and pretending a certain amount of ignorance
about the workings of fairytales

there will be critical moments when one word from
rose would change the story's plot. but she knows
her role and will hold her tongue. history

is the thorny realm of rich powerful princes

in the meantime rose can play games with trolls and
witches. her prince will tolerate it as long as
she doesn't cross him. as long as her game
doesn't interfere with his

and if she wants she can even make a sport of
equal height between normals & dwarfs. he will
understand. she needs to do something for
amusement—as long as the dwarfs
remain dwarfs

he will even allow her a wolf or two

thus our gal rose needn't concern herself
with the eternal sleep threatening the kingdom
she is assured resurrection by the local
sorcerer who offers happy endings
at a discount

CHAIR AFFAIR

the chair bites me. angrily i kick it

the chair wheezes every time
i sit down in it

i have decided i hate this chair
even though i need its support

the chair moves into an awkward angle every
time i get up so i am forced to look at it
before i sit down again

hard little round metallic doo-doos
keep coming out of the chair
causing me to watch my step

i have offered a truce. the loss of 25
pounds. the chair scoffs

the chair doctor states it will take
3 months and over four thousand dollars to
cure the chair

today my horoscope said avoid
recalcitrant chairs

when i came in from lunch
i found another butt in my chair

"chairs are the true plague of mankind"
— Chairman Mao

91

FAT LENA

She riding in the car next to her husband he be
rubber-neckin' at all the pretty womens age no
object and Fat Lena feel herself gettin' fatter by
the minute wonderin' why he don't reserve his
lust for her cuz they married anyway and she like
to fuck as much as he do even if she new at it and
not nearly as experienced but he want a virgin
and that what he got Fat Lena never had a boy
break her cherry till he come along she had a few
hold her hand and squeeze up all around her and
two or three try a kiss and one day Fat Lena go to
the liquor store for her Mama this young man just
come up on her and feel her titty where it ought
to be but there's just barely enough to grab hold
to and he tear the button off her jumper and ran
away when she scream in a fear totally new to her
not knowing why she was supposed to be afraid of
that skinny little ugly brown boy so that was when
Mama began to explain sex sort of and Fat Lena
married at last and moved out and all day she lay
up and watch television and eat junk and wait for
her husband to come home and maybe they go
somewhere and do something but lately she not
so happy as she was cuz he started eyeballing
other womens and not even hiding it from her he
whistles and carries on like she's not there or is
just another man and it hurts her feelings real
bad but Fat Lena she don't know how to tell him

and one day he pull up at a stop light and while he lookin' off in another direction an old man steps off the curb and the old man catch sight of Lena and he grin a big grin at her and lick his tongue out at her as he passes in front of the car and Lena grinned back at him and suddenly she feel good and warm deep inside like God done told her there's hope for her yet.

NO WOMAN'S LAND

they trample on my sensitivity
goose-step thru streets of my affection
line me up before the firing squad of insecurity, shoot me down

when the smoke clears
my corpse interred
they sing my praises in a hymn

love politics—a legislature of pricks

they pass bogus bills of understanding
table my lusts in committee
refuse to acknowledge my plea for justice

before supreme court of need

when the fires die
they toss my ashes to the wind
moan prayers

administrative coup—détente for them, defeat for me

they demilitarize the zone of my thighs
napalm my dreams of black womanhood
overkill my illusions in a pushbutton mechanized fuck-session

when the dust settles
my hopes float face-up in the
river tears

martial law—immediate withdrawal?

no white flag of truce
no surrender

SAPPHIRE AS ARTIST IN THE WORLD

—after William H. Gass

The work such woman does in the world works on her . . . her
movements her perceptions her loves. Life is intolerable in a society that does not
value/want her gift; especially when it does not want the vision she must espouse
in the act of putting herself in the world thru art. What does Sapphire envision?
Her innate loveliness of which she may be defensive or insecure. But if she seeds
her self-doubt in a nurturing self-love she may harvest the rapture of creation.
Otherwise she may fill herself with hate, but will her skin contain it? Hate blurs.
Certainly she cannot create when her vision is blurred/out-of-sync/arhythmic.
Rhythm is a state of concentration so complete it leaves her defenseless, opens to
all in tune with it. Intonation is her other means/meaning into sensation by which
her faculties embrace/subvert. To achieve satiation upon embracing she must *see*
the world she enlarges (with her art) clearly if not without fear. She is its lover
and she must excite it until its richness rises in response to her Afro-centric beauty
perceived at last. To openly hate and fear her lover is to invite rape. She must see
the hardness in the blood, yet recognize the hardness as required for effective
penetration/dialogue. Therefore she is the natural enemy of social oppression/
impotence. She resists the aesthetic softness of a society that would sublimate/
smother her spirit. In this context her subversion is catholic, but given sufficient
direction/education her willfulness undermines everything false with exacting
precision. In the end her society will reject or even destroy her. History is clear on
this point. To insure her place in the world Sapphire must make her art her
revolution. And in so making she must remain undaunted, without compromise.
She must be aware of the power which extends thru her bones, the profound
stubborn belief in the absolute importance of her vision.

RAPE

—thanx, Kika Warfield

i am here to help you

he laughed. and his partner laughed. she squeezed
her palms/triggers. their uniforms bled
the laughter became screams of horror and she
dragged the bodies of the white blond cop and
his chinese bunky down stairs
and buried them in her eyes/hatred
sprang up and blossomed

talk about it

tell me every detail, said the doctor
they broke in on me. every detail. they took me
in the bedroom, one at a time. next detail
i was scared they'd find my purse—i lied about
having no money. detail, detail. they undressed me,
asked me to tell them how it felt. did it feel
good? yes. did you cum? they were gentle lovers
did you cum? yes. both times? yes

the boyfriend

came in. she was feeling shrunken dirty suicide
she hadn't douched. the wetness still pouring
out/a sticky riverlet on her inner thighs
he got indignant. why didn't she call the police
why didn't she call her mama. why didn't she die

97

fighting. she remained silent. he asked her where
it happened. she showed him the spot. he
pulled down his pants, forced her back onto the sheets
i haven't cleaned up, she whined. but he was
full saddle hard dicking and cumming torrents

the two burglars

kicked the door in. she woke. she thought, he's
drunk again. she slipped into her thin pink
gown, got up and went to see. it wasn't him. we
have guns, the dark one announced
there's no one here but me and the kids she said

there was little

for them to steal. the dark one took her into
the bedroom while his partner searched. he turned
out the lights and stripped. he laid her gently on
the bed. this is my name. when you cum, call
my name. she agreed. and he entered. your pussy's
hot and tight. where's your old man? he's
a fool not to be here with you. you're pretty
you're soft. you fuck good. kiss me. and she did
as told. we don't want to hurt you. you like
the way i kiss. tell the truth. it's good,
she said and after a while she moaned his name

the other one

came in and took off his clothes in the dark
i'm really sorry to do this, he said, but
i can't help myself. strange, she thought. such
polite rapists. i wonder if they'll kill me
somehow i must make them care enough not
to kill me. he told her his name and sucked
hungry at her nipples, parted her legs
he was very thick long hard. his friend's seed
eased the pain. i want your tongue he said
give me your tongue. she gave and gave
jesus! he cried and shot into her, long spastic jerks
he trembled and fell into her arms. shit
that was good

in the kitchen

her few valuables were piled neatly mid-floor
she promised not to call the police
what could they do, save her?
the other one, the jesus-man took her typewriter
and put it back, and all the other stuff they
had planned to take. even the television

here is my number, said the dark one
when you get lonely, call

and she walked

them to the door. the dark one took her in his
arms
kissed her goodbye

she waited

until she was sure they wouldn't
come back and kill

she picked up the phone

and made the mistake of thinking the world
would understand

100

CONFESSIONS NOIRES

i am afraid of telephones

one of my greatest highs is city driving
before sunrise after rain, listening

frequently the likeness of my first husband
masks the faces of our children calling to mind
an inscription i made on a photo—some hogshit
about his being my first my last

i hate dresses

i have no fear of needles
only users of needles

101

the only thang i'm hooked on these days
is money. withdrawal pangs are constant

i'm not the type, said i
all women are the type said he
and if you're not it's going to be quite a
pleasure finding out what type you are

my worst nightmares are about telephones

once i pulled off a robbery
got away with the goods, then, like a fool
gave them to my lover-of-the-moment
to impress him

Ann Petry wrote my life's story published the year
i was born

i prefer commercials over programming
black and white over color
informed silence over ignorant applause

i pray only on airplanes

occasionally one of my dreams
comes true

once in a while i pass myself going
in the other direction

102   *i am afraid of the light*
        at the end of a poem

DEATH THREAT #1, OR HOW I LEARNED TO STOP WORRYING AND LOVE THE BOMB

A Performance Monologue by Dee Russell

"YEAH, THIS IS FOR DEE RUSSELL,
THANKS FOR LETTING ME KNOW WHERE I CAN FIND YOU
'CAUSE I'M GONNA KILL YOU, YOU FUCKING BLACK NIGGER BITCH
FUCKING CUNT! YOUR ART SUCKS AND SO DO YOU, AND YOU KNOW WHAT?
YOU'RE DEAD, NIGGER!"

This really happened in San Francisco, California. A man called my hotline, my "ArtSlave Entertainment Calendar," an up-to-the-minute listing of where I perform, where my "Handbag Art" is sold, superficial tabloid gossip, my philosophy . . . a cute, two-minute long announcement.

That man listened to my hotline and vomited hate on the phone tape. I accessed my messages quite early that day—woman's intuition be damned! I recall my jaw dropped, I gasped and gulped, my stomach felt ill, hollow. I cried. I called my best friend. I cried. I felt that day I would truly DIE, perhaps shot from the kitchen window, my throat slashed as I attempted to eat a burrito, a fire-bomb on my doorstep?!! I cried.

I was led to the HATE CRIME SQUAD, police detectives committed to solving crimes based on race or sex. One reasonably kind detective said, "That's the price of fame, you should get used to it. This happens all the time in show business." I cried. The phone company placed a "trap" on my hotline, a hook to snare that deadly fish. He never called back. I cried. "He raped my soul," I cried.

I didn't feel safe at night anymore. No more late night power strolls. I bleached and dyed my thick, healthy dark hair a most vile shade of green, growing it brittle and damaged. Anything not to resemble the dark-haired, vulnerable me that was victimized by that ugly voice. I developed an eating disorder, yes, black women get eating disorders. I was the Queen of the Queasy Stomach, a lean, clean, mean, regurgitating machine.

I have changed forevermore. I cry easily now, at the drop of a hat. I listen to my stomach when judging newcomers. When I planned on using the death threat audio as "art," on the advice of my kind and gentle "sister-girl" therapist, a few "friends" said that I was giving the situation more power. "Don't talk about it so much," they said, thinking that they were kind. One man actually laughed when told of the death threat, commenting, "Well, didn't you expect something like this to happen?"

The majority of the folks I came in contact with didn't know how to comfort me, which I perceived as, "Black women are not soft, no matter what happens, they are strong as steel, they can take care of themselves, they're tough as a truck, they can handle it, they deserve it, they're rough and tough and they don't cry."

Dehumanized, I grew extremely paranoid, hyper-sensitive to American society's racial flaws. I trusted all people less, particularly men, and I certainly held no open arms welcome for new white male pals, since it was a white male voice that helped screw up my head, heart, and soul. I slipped further into paranoia.

I mind my own business and they call me a bitch. They touch my odd-looking hair without asking my permission, then they call me a bitch when I say, "Please don't touch me." They say I'm a bitch because I take care of my soul, they call me a bitch because I win video awards and receive grants for solo work. No matter what I do, they call me a bitch. I no longer crave their approval, they can't help me, anyway. Sad, stupid, art-hag situations. Theater, cocktails, opening-night receptions, film/video festivals, pathetic poetry readings. In I walk knowing no matter how many grants, or Hollywood video awards I've been presented with, I'm THE BITCH. . . .

In this business of show, show business, I am considered a success. They all crave my boho-bitchy-hip brand of approval, that play/party/reading/video shoot is a happening thang because a strong black art bitch is here to make that quota, get that grant, be the bitch!

Only blondes, only white women are allowed the right and privilege to be fragile in this American scream? I am brave, oh, pretending to be brave. Aren't black women allowed to cry when they are hurt in America? Aren't black women allowed to cry when they are hurt by America? I am a small black woman with no children who cries all the time. "You don't see crying black women on American TV or the movies," I cry.
I cry because I am afraid of America.
I cry.
I feel my art hasn't made a difference.
I cry because I am afraid.
My question is, suicide or Paris?

105

FORUM III: SELF-REVELATION: THE ART OF REWRITING PERSONAL HISTORY

Dorothy Allison
Sapphire
Cheryl C. Brodie
Christine Cobaugh
Sue Martin

For survivors of rape, incest and domestic violence, the process of self-disclosure in narrative, poetry and visual art can be a way out of the victim/siege mentality. By reframing the past, artists and writers change the terms of their relationship to their experiences. The panelists discuss transformation through creative expression, and the process by which the social repression of information about abuse perpetuates the cycles of violence. They also discuss their efforts as activists to promote public awareness about sexual violence through their work.

Amy Scholder

Dorothy Allison

I'm forty-three years old. Twenty years ago, in Tallahassee, Florida, I went to my first consciousness-raising group. It was a lesbian consciousness-raising group. It was extraordinarily important to me. I was almost at the point where I was ready to give up. I was suicidal, I was madly in love with a completely bitchy, mean, little girl who was not giving me anything I needed. I was working myself to death for the social security administration of the state of Florida. I was helping to publish a feminist magazine; I was working in the child-care center and the rape crisis center. I was doing those six-meetings-a-week-you-don't-need-to-sleep-anyway blues and I went into that Sunday afternoon CR group and I sat down and everybody started talking and mostly they were talking about other women who were not in the group that they had recently broken up with. But one of the women in the group started talking about her father and how she really needed to tell people that she hated him and that she dreamed every night of going home to kill him and that the dreams had become so vivid that they were the only things she looked forward to. So I said, "I'll do yours if you'll do mine." I was joking but I was also half-serious.

That was the beginning of being able to talk about how I had grown up. I was taught never to tell anyone outside the family what's going on, not just because it's shameful but because it is literally physically damaging and dangerous to you. I was told, If they find out, they'll take you away and you'll go and wind up in county detention and you will spend the rest of your life in and out of jail. It does not matter that this is rape and that you didn't ask for it. It doesn't matter because you are who you are. You are our kid, you're part of this family. If they find out, you're dead. And if you kill him you're dead because they'll put you in county detention. Little girls do not kill their fathers and get away with it. I was taught to be very quiet, very polite in public, talk to the Sunday school ladies with a good diction, try to get that scholarship and get the hell out of home, which is exactly what I did.

And I did it so successfully that I convinced myself that only poor men rape their daughters, only poor men beat their daughters, and only poor women let them. And I believed that grown-up middle class girls were a different creature, that that didn't happen in their families. So there was another reason not to tell. But that woman in that beanbag chair wasn't just middle-class, Christ God, she was a failed upper-class kid. And in telling me about her life she was telling me about my life. She was telling me about how when she was a girl, she used to fight with her little brother about who was going to have to sleep next to the door, which is something my sisters and I did until I left home and they had to deal alone. She was telling me about sleeping over with girlfriends, not because you want to be friends or even because you want to lick their pussies, but because then you won't be sleeping at home. And she was telling me about growing up believing that being beaten is normal, that being backhanded is everyday, that being called names is a regular part of it, that everybody does it, we just don't talk about it in public. We thought we were freaks. We thought we were monsters from another planet and what we found out in talking to each other, and eventually we found four or five others and put ourselves together, is that the planet is earth and that the family is a prison camp for a great many of us.

I didn't start writing, or at least I didn't start keeping the writing, until 1974 when I published a poem. Everything I wrote before then—ten years of journals, ten years of poems and short stories—I burned because I was afraid somebody would read them. And always in the back of my mind there were my mother's whispers: They'll send you to the detention, you'll wind up in county home. You don't want to do that.

I'm forty-three years old. Sometimes I dream I'm a thirteen-year-old girl locked behind bars with her pussy hurting and not knowing how to talk to anybody. And sometimes I still dream that I go down to Florida with a shotgun, broken down and packed in a suitcase.

When I set out to write the novel that I published last spring [*Bastard Out of Carolina*], I wanted to do two things. I wanted to create the family that I deeply loved and was not saved by, and I wanted to put in print everything that I understood that happens in a violent family where incest is taking place. I wanted to show people that everyday life is everyday life, that mostly they come to get you at night and when your mother's working late and that most of your struggle as a child is about trying not to believe you're the monster that that person is convincing you you are. That most of the struggle for incest children is to tell yourself that you are a real person and that this thing that is happening to you is not something you're making happen, because when I was a kid I thought I was doing it. I thought, if only I was a little better, a little smarter, a little meaner, a little faster, or maybe even a better Christian, this wouldn't be happening. So I wrote as strong a story as I could about a young girl who is slowly convinced that she is a monster and who is not saved by the people she loves. What's been missing for me in talking to other survivors is how I have always felt about my mother. I don't need to tell you what my stepfather did to me as a child, and I have worked through so much of it that it's no longer desperately necessary for me to say it, except that I have to be kind of matter of fact, you know, that "I'm not going to be ashamed so I'm going to say to you 'the motherfucker fucked me from the time I was five.'" I do that, but I don't want to talk about that so much as what happens when you really love your little sisters, but you make them sleep by the door. And you really love your mother, but you hate it that she doesn't come home from work right away, that she's an hour and a half late and you've got to survive that hour and a half without her. And you really love her but you can't understand why she doesn't take you out of there, go anywhere, live in any condition but not the one you're in. I know absolutely that my mother loved me and loved my sisters and that she did everything she could understand to do to try to save us. But I also know that she had no idea of what was really going on, partly because she was telling lies to herself to stay sane, and partly because we were lying to her to save her and to save ourselves, and that becomes a habit.

My sisters do not remember our childhood. One of the roles that I play is giving it back to them, and one of the problems is that I write fiction, so I take little pieces of real things that happened to us and I move sometimes very far away from it, and they don't know the difference. What I've had to do this past year is sit down with them and say, "That page is true. It didn't happen to

109

me, though, it happened to you." And I do not know anything that has been as hard as that. My sisters do not allow my stepfather in their home; they do not allow him to be alone with their children. In point of fact, my younger sister doesn't allow any men to be alone with her children. And the hard thing I had to explain to her is, it isn't just men. I had to tell her about all the women I found after I left home, that the world is a bigger, meaner, more complicated place than they ever told us, and that the tools for dealing with it are real but we have to make them up as we go along. One of the reasons I write is to make up those tools, to show my sisters a few of the things I've learned and take back from them the things that they can teach me. And because I just got a letter from that woman in the beanbag chair and she's living in Iowa and she has a daughter and the first thing she said to me was, "I don't dream about shotguns anymore, I just think about it now and again in the daylight."

110

Sapphire

I didn't remember I was an incest survivor until I was thirty-eight years old. I was in a classroom in the South Bronx and I looked out the window and instead of urban decay I saw a park with green grass, wooden picnic benches and tables and me as a child, and a man, who I know is my uncle. It was a "visual flashback." Sylvia Fraser, author of *My Father's House,* says "We tend to think of memory as only residing in the mind, but the body has specific memories too."

Even now, when I think of abuse, I think, I must be crazy to say something like that, like, my father raped me, practically before I could walk. I think to myself, He couldn't have, It's all in my mind, I must be nuts! But I know that until I can accept the impossible—that my "normal," upstanding father stuck his penis in me when I was a child—I will think I am crazy. I will think I am losing my mind.

This is a quote from *Father-Daughter Incest,* a book by Judith Herman: "A relationship was observed between the age of onset, duration and degree of violence of the abused and the extent to which the memory had been repressed." I used to have body memories, i.e., feelings in my body with no visual pictures. It was if my body were releasing information, trying to tell me something. I guess my body had been trying to tell me something all my life, but I had learned not to listen to my body because I had come to view it as the enemy: something to be controlled and contained; a source of shame, embarrassment, pain, and the reason I was raped. Intellectually, I know now that I was raped because my father chose to act out his sickness on me. But my child self felt this happened to me because I have a female body. Trying to accept my body is still one of my hardest tasks.

In 1986, my older brother was murdered. He was a schizophrenic. And I believe that his schizophrenia was a response to the abuse he suffered as a child. His body had this information, these memories that he couldn't accept. His concept of what it meant to be a man didn't allow him to let in that information.

111

So he went "crazy"; he withdrew totally from reality. One of his hallucinations was that the devil was after him. And at his funeral I remember looking at my father and realizing, there's the devil.

Accepting the possibility that I had been abused as a child was the beginning of a journey back to myself—the self I had tried to kill three times, tried to drown in drugs, alcohol, food, and fantasy. "Mickey Mouse was a Scorpio" was the first poem in which I wrote about myself in the first person as an incest survivor. I think it was important for me to get up in front of people and read it without shame, knowing there was nothing wrong with me, that I hadn't done anything wrong. I first read it in 1989, at an event coordinated by Allen Wright and Bill Wright of Other Countries, a black gay men's writing group. The evening was called A Page from a Black Child's Diary.

112

MICKEY MOUSE WAS A SCORPIO

the night was no light,
black.
he came in
light cracking the night
stuck in the doorway
of dark
deep hard.
my father,
lean in blue & white striped pajamas,
snatches my pajama bottoms off
grabs me by my little skinny knees
& drives his dick in.
i scream
i scream
no one hears except my sister
who becomes no one 'cause she didn't hear.
years later i become no one 'cause it didn't happen
but it's night now & it's happening,
a train with razor blades for wheels
is riding thru my asshole
iron hands saw at my knees
i'm gonna die
i'm gonna die
blood, semen & shit gush from my cracked ass.
my mother, glad not to be the one,
comes in when it's over to wash me.
she is glad glad,
satanic glad.

she brings her hand up from between my legs &
smears shit, semen & blood over my mouth,
"Now she'll know what it's like to have a baby," she
howls.
drugged night so black
you could paint with it,
no moon no stars no god
the night stick smashes my spinal cord,
my legs
bleeding bandages of light
fall off.
let me go
let me go
don't tell me about god & good little girls
i want to live
i want to live
my cells crack open like glass
the bells are tolling for me
my name disintegrates in the night
God's a lie
this can't be true.
M-I-C-K-E-Y- M-O-U-S-E
mother is house (we have a nice house
California ranch style)
brother is the nail
we drive thru your heart
do it
do it to her, brother.
M-I-C-K-E-Y M-O-U-S-EEE
mouse is in the house

running thru my vagina
& out my nose
saucer-eyed bucktooth child
Betsy Wetsy
brown bones
electrocuted.
Tiny Tears
that never dry
hopscotch
hickory dock
the mouse fell off
the clock
the farmer takes Jill down the well
& all the king's horses
& all the king's men
can't put that baby together again.
crooked man
crooked man
pumpkin eater
childhood stealer.

115

Cheryl C. Brodie

My determination to speak through my work came on a very specific day. At noon, January 19, 1987, one of my dearest friends committed suicide. She hanged herself.

We had worked in a group of five women. It was my first experience of a women's collective. We were dealing with incest. Judy was never fully able to place responsibility with the perpetrator, even though she was an infant when the molestation began. I had never been able to cry or express rage. I was living in a perpetual haze of rationality—still trying to prove I wasn't bad, crazy, or responsible for my own victimization. Judy's death unleashed emotions that had lain dormant and toxic for thirty-five years.

At her funeral, family member after family member bemoaned Judy's instability, her mental illness—the very same people who molested her or were complicit in the act. That day I promised Judy and myself that I would never be silenced again. I began channeling my tears and outrage. I met other women who were doing the same. All of us were resolved to be seen and to be heard— to be active in our own lives.

I was raised in a working class home. My father was active in the working world, in the union; and he was an alcoholic. He raped, beat, and molested my mother, my sister and me. My mother allied herself with my father, betraying and blaming my sister and me. My sister and I were pitted against one another. My father preferred me to her. We learned that women were competition, adversaries, and not to be trusted.

Silence surrounded our home rendering my father's acts sacred and unstoppable. His violence moved from the private sphere to the more public, as he began beating my mother in the yard in full view of the neighbors, without fear of reprisal. Eventually he began to throw her in the car and take her to locations where she was held hostage as he forced her to watch him perform sexually with other women, beating her all the while.

I never stopped speaking in that home although I was punished severely. Somewhere inside I understood that my mother's silence had crushed her spirit. I refused to be deadened so completely. I confronted my father about the abuse, incest, alcoholism, and insanity. My persistence in speaking was an act of survival in a world where law enforcement would enter our home, isolate me as the vocal one, and admonish me to pray. There was nothing they could or would do. My parents identified me as crazy, as a child who never really wanted to be their child, thereby forfeiting any protection. Eventually, I began to believe I deserved everything I got.

Ironically, there's a rich tradition in working class communities—my family included—of women talking among themselves. I was fascinated by their speech, the weaving of stories. I would listen for hours, absorbing the rhythms of their language. They debated politics among themselves and with the men. However, I learned an important distinction: these women talked prolifically to each other, but never spoke publicly. They were confined to the domestic sphere.

The first time I spoke in public was spontaneous. *Roe vs. Wade* was about to be decided. I was attending a weekly Sunday Catholic mass at our local parish. The priest handed out petitions to be signed en masse protesting the imminent passage of legal abortion. I was instinctively outraged. To be honest, I had no opinion on abortion. In fact, I knew very little of the arguments or circumstances surrounding the controversy. It seemed remote from the world I lived in. I simply rebelled at the coercion implied by all of us held hostage in the pews, signing by rote. I also recall wondering angrily what he—a celibate man—knew of abortion. I began to walk out. I was confronted by the parish priest. I replied vehemently that I would not participate in anything presented with so little balanced information.

Fifteen years passed before I found that voice again. I spent much of that time trying to be the woman I believed I was born to be. I could never quite squeeze myself into the crate that had been so insistently constructed for me. I would sink to levels of depression that consumed weeks and months in which I

117

sleepwalked through my life, dying to still those outspoken words that had caused so much pain and punishment.

When I decided to further my education, my working class family, who were fiercely proud of their innate intelligence and lack of education, disapproved. The women feared that I was throwing my future away—they believed that by going to college I was systematically destroying my marriage and, along with it, any rational means of financial support. I cannot express the courage that step took: I saw college as a place other people attended, people who were geniuses. I couldn't believe it when I was admitted. The first year I was constantly worried about being revealed as a fraud. I made the choice to go to college with a wildly vague hope of finding a place in the world where I could begin to speak once again and live as fully as possible.

It was not until Judy's death in 1987 that I took seriously my potential as an artist. My work began on a very personal level. Gradually I began to understand the social and political context of the events in my life. I learned about the women's movement only seven years ago, as I entered a world of educated women.

When I prepared for this speech, I faced questions and dilemmas that threatened to silence me once more. Through this process of preparation, I have made a commitment to myself to find my way back home—reaching out to women who have never heard the word feminist, or if they have, believe that being an empowered woman will kill them. As a feminist artist, I need to find a voice that speaks to my fears as well as theirs.

I believe we need to subvert the notion of authority or expertise for women participating on panels, and begin to view panels as opportunities for active listening, for increased dialogue, as well as for respecting our separate truths. It's an opportunity to include all of us—to speak in terms that are not exclusive—while challenging long-entrenched practices both within and outside the many movements that are feminist.

There are many women who don't attend these conferences because they feel they don't belong in these rooms, that their voices and concerns are not represented. Many of us who do attend sit silently, never making a statement or asking a question for fear of not knowing the right words, for fear of being misunderstood, for fear of hearing her own voice in a room she's never learned to claim as her own. I'm one of those women who rarely attend and when I do, never speak.

If we want to effect change, we need to be willing to listen to others' experiences; we need to question barriers of race and class, jealousies among ourselves, the notion of specialness and privilege that bind many of us in a drive to succeed in a world that allows only a few to achieve recognition.

119

"Pear Box: Letter to My Father # I" took place at the end of twenty-eight days (the days of my menstrual cycle) in which I wrote, or attempted to write, a letter to my father every day. Five friends and I went to the beach to burn the letters in a pear crate. I had sandblasted the letters *P E A R* in four thick shards of broken glass. The letters, rearranged, also spell the word *rape*. A wave surrounded the rock and washed the basket with the glass letters into the ocean. The basket was found upright on the beach with a cone of sand in the center. At first I experienced loss, followed by exhilaration and a strong sense of having been cleansed. We proceeded to burn the twenty-eight letters in the pear crate. The relics that remained were the two charred ends of the crate—folded out like an open book, a new chapter about to begin.

"Pear Box: Letter to My Father #4" began as a letter to my mother and ended as a letter to my father. Through this work, I began to understand the concept of woman as both victim and victimizer. On the inside cover, hand-stamped repeatedly are the words, "If I should die before I wake." The strip of film inset in the ironing board is a repeated image of me at five years old, holding and feeding an infant. Behind me is a domestic scene from our housewarming party in 1958. The counter is filled with beer bottles and my father is framed in the doorway. Transparencies sandwiched in the acrylic frame inside the front door read, "'I have a surprise for you,' he said," and "Do you know the muffin man?" The text is a reminder that perpetrators are colleagues, husbands, uncles, grandfathers, brothers, the man next door. The tarnished silver tray holds a red pear with a bee pinned to it. Tufts of my cut hair lay at the base of the fruit. The intended letter to my mother was inspired by "I Stand Here Ironing" by Tillie Olson.

"Pear Box: Letter to My Father #5" is the final piece in this series. It is a testimony to my experience as a child in the 1950s, a testament to the way women are trapped by the weight of silence, and a protest against censorship. It is also a reminder of the era of McCarthyism. The text "Testimony, Testify, Testament" stems from the Latin root, testis, which means to witness. These words

121

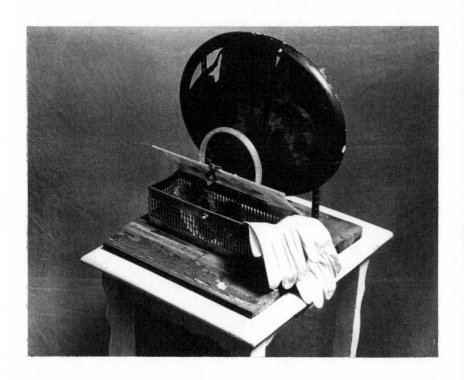

refer to an ancient custom of men swearing oaths on one another's testicles; men continue to protect each other, attempting to censor or discredit anyone who questions the validity of patriarchy.

Christine Cobaugh

I have worked in the battered women's movement since 1985. My
primary job is community education, outreach, and prevention. I am also a
photographer. I was in a violent relationship for about nine years, which has
impacted the rest of my life and is what got me into the field of working with
battered women and children. I have been a feminist for a long time, and my
batterer was a peace activist and also very active in progressive politics, so this
community was not a safe place for me to go at that time.

My batterer destroyed a lot of my photographs. I left Los Angeles
and moved to the Bay Area where he followed me. (It's quite common for
batterers to track down and chase their partners.) As a formerly battered woman
and as an artist, it was a difficult and challenging time in my life. The images that
I was working on were cathartic, very personal, and yet at the same time they
were very distant from me. I couldn't allow myself to feel what the images were
describing. I think I had to do that for survival.

125

My photographs here are essentially self-portraits. The woman in the
photographs appears to be dead. There's a sense of isolation, loneliness. Figures
in the background are reminiscent of those who had been there, or passed her by,
or ignored her. The experience of shooting these was a whole other element. I
was dragging around these bodies on the beach and people were following me. So
it created a crowd of mostly men and children wherever I went. At the time, even
though I knew these images were powerful for me, I couldn't name what they
were about. Later, I started to re-experience the hopelessness, the sadness, the
isolation, the anger, and the rage that was just below the surface.

I didn't know at the time that these photographs were the beginning
of self-disclosure. People around me, the few people who did see these images in
the beginning, never asked me questions, never named what they saw or felt,
never brought to my attention that there might be something else going on here
other than these "interesting" two-dimensional images. Self-disclosure has been a

powerful tool for my own healing process, and I see its value when I work with battered women: to create a safe place, and encourage them to start that self-disclosure process, which is often the first step toward creating a whole, new life.

127

Sue Martin

My major theme and concern about violence against women is that it is about silence—the silencing of our voices, our power, and our souls. Even though we are starting to see images and writing and some movies about violence against women, there is still a pervasive silence about the truth of that violence in terms of how we deal with it personally, with each other, and with society as a whole. I had participated in part of that silence for many decades because I did not know that I had been a victim of male violence. That silence went deep, all the way to the unconscious. I believe this happens because of the constructs and the values in this society. Our culture will go to any lengths to make sure that we are disconnected from ourselves as women, to make sure that we are disconnected particularly from our bodies, and that we deny and question our experiences.

In this culture, women in particular are taught to embrace addiction. I talk about addiction because it has had a very strong role in my life, in silencing the abuse and even my knowledge of abuse. I am talking about chemical addictions (alcohol, drugs, and nicotine) and about eating disorders (anorexia and bulimia). I'm also talking about what I'm still struggling with today, and that is work addiction—the belief that if I just do enough, I will be okay, I will be safe.

Seventeen years ago, I began working in the women's movement, particularly, on issues of violence against women. Somewhere deep inside of me I knew I needed to work on these issues, but I didn't know why. I grew up with seven brothers, and I knew that it wasn't great, but I didn't really know why. My survival mechanism as a child was to be very smart and very quick, because if I could talk it, if I could think it, then I would survive. All those years I successfully held down the knowledge of abuse, contained it and tried to void it. It was only when I started working on my addictions and moving beyond them that I began to change. I was then able to take up the artistic process to get further information and go deeper into the recovery process.

129

Through this process I came to know that I was physically and sexually abused as a child. It was the only way I could access that information. The creative process I use, the Life/Art Process, is based on the authentic movement of the body—and our bodies do not lie. Because abuse is also about relationships with other people, I believe that healing can't just happen in therapy; it has to have a public, visible expression if we're going to heal ourselves and our culture.

What has been so exciting and important for me in this process has been doing art as part of building community. I have used works of art for educational purposes in the battered women's movement; I'd like to see this done on a much larger scale. I want to find a way to create and show art that depicts the terror and rage and healing on a very direct level. I want to make the artistic process available to all women—to find ways for more women to be able to express themselves and our collective truths.

130

DISCUSSION

COMMENT: I wonder if you could comment on the complexities of the situation for women who are introduced to orgasm at the time of sexual abuse. That was my experience, and it has made my sexuality especially difficult to talk about, because the issue of pleasure is not a straightforward one. I was abused sexually by almost all the men in my family, and at some point I was having orgasms during nonconsensual sex. But no one ever seems to want to deal with what happens to the way you talk about abuse, how blame gets involved if you say that at the same time, I didn't want it/ask for it, *and* I was sexually aroused.

DOROTHY ALLISON: I want to thank you very much for talking about this. The thing about being a survivor that we rarely get to face in public and talk to other survivors about is how complicated sexuality becomes. I got paid three dollars for sex a couple of times, but mostly I got peace. I was the peacemaker in my family.

I can remember being sent in because he was in a rampage and if Dorothy went in there with him for half an hour everything would be fine, nobody else would get yelled at, the doors wouldn't get broken, the bills would get paid. I learned to do that so well that when I became sexually active, which for me came very late (I basically learned not to do sex), I had this trick that I had learned with him of shutting down. With my women lovers, I would guess what they wanted before they could tell me because that's the only thing I had learned to do. I never had a clue what I wanted. Nobody had ever given me any place in which I could learn that, and it's taken me most of my life to learn it.

The other thing that's really difficult to talk about is that I grew up associating sexual satisfaction with violence and with being afraid, and that I basically became incapable of sexual response if there was not some element of fear. I was, therefore, much more attracted to women who were abrupt or just mean, and much more attracted to S/M, to bondage, partly because of the fear and the sexual violence, but also because it was absolutely under control. I really liked having my girlfriends tied up. They weren't going to do anything unpredictable if I knew that they could not move. It became, in fact, a way for me to learn to be sexual. Which is a process of finding out for yourself what your real desire is. No one can tell you those things about yourself, and it's a goddamned long and complicated process. I swear to God, it's like swimming through mud and you have to keep waving the mud out of the way constantly so you can see down into what is really a very buried sexual self.

I have also learned that I want it to be over. I want to reach the point where I have got it figured out and it has healed and it has stopped. I am damn tired of feeling like I'm grown up, I'm in control, it's OK now, and having it come back on me in a completely new, unpredictable way, which is continually my experience, especially around sexuality and situations of threat. I cannot ever seem to get to a place where there is not a new surprise, where there is not something I did not know. And I'm not talking about lost memory; I'm talking about things that are hidden in my body. I'll give you an example: When I began to be able to be sexual, when I began to be able to have orgasms with other

131

women that did not involve elaborate scenarios, I suddenly developed a response that, when I orgasmed, I hit somebody. I would automatically start punching. And it was so uncontrollable that for a couple of years I stopped having sex unless I could get myself tied up because once I managed to break my girlfriend's nose. When I worked through that, I still had a response for years of shaking continually whenever I would get sexually excited. I'm not saying this because some of it is weird and some of it is funny, but because I didn't see these things coming, and they keep coming.

We have a new baby. He's two months old. When I first saw him, held him, realized how fragile, how unbelievably tender a baby's body and skin is—I never knew that in my own body before—I stopped being able to jerk off, I stopped being able to have sex for about three weeks. It was like I had to process this new information that my body didn't have. It was information about me. What I've realized is that you have to be patient, both with yourself and with the other people in your life. I am at war with the idea that incest survivors cannot have a sexuality, and that they cannot name their own sexuality and do any damn thing they need to get it. There are too many people in this society who want us to give it up, and I think that's just about societal control. It's very dangerous when a woman figures out what she wants and knows how to go about getting it.

SAPPHIRE: As an incest survivor, one of the major issues around sexuality was control, and I think that S/M and, primarily, prostitution provided for me an arena in which I *felt* I was in control, and also where I could recreate the absolute terror. There was a need for me to recreate this terror that I must have experienced as a child, and I would do this by putting myself in situations where I was totally vulnerable, where I couldn't defend myself. I don't think I consciously planned this, but over and over I'd be in situations where people could kill me, where I was totally vulnerable.

When I was in my late teens I was with a group of sex workers and they were discussing a disgusting older man who was hanging around these young prostitutes, and it turned out to be my father. This was again some insight into why I would become this type of person. I thought I was rebelling with drugs and prostitution against the culture at large and my family, not realizing that I had recreated the very self that he wanted most, even though I'm sure he never would have admitted it. It took many years to begin to find a real sexuality and a sexuality that wasn't based on control, fear, and terror.

QUESTION: What is your response to women, particularly mothers, who deny abuse in the family, or defend the abuser?

SUE MARTIN: I'm continually shocked by the level of denial that women live under. I have a phenomenal amount of rage and anger toward my mother. And I ask myself, Why did she have eleven children and almost die in the process? What was she doing? I also know that she was a victim in her own right. I don't know about her own childhood or what happened to her physically, but I have a lot of sadness for her life today, for what has been true in her life and for what she never got a chance to experience. It's a dilemma for women today. We are trying to come to a point of honesty in our own lives and hold ourselves and each other accountable for abusive behavior, and yet we have such different access to resources than our mothers had. It is a very difficult and painful process. Somehow we must find creative ways to break through all forms of denial.

133

SAPPHIRE: I'm angry at my mother, very angry. She had a hard life, but she didn't have to turn me over to my father in the way that she did. I understand what she went through—maybe I don't, I mean you can never understand what another person goes through—but I'm very, very angry that she disappeared on me. It's a deep source of grief. I talk a lot about the sexually perpetrating parent, in my case, my father. But by being silent and passive, she hurt me, too. I was deprived of any positive female role model, of knowing what a fighter could be, and what a strong woman could be. I had to find that out as an adult.

It's important for me to speak about my family because we were a nuclear family. And this is often the model that is held up to African Americans as normal, healthy, what we should seek to attain. Now, it is not necessarily the model our ancestors in Africa followed: Africans had many different types of families, including marriages between females, as well as polyandrous and polygamous unions. All this information was lost to us during slavery, and we were left with our masters' lifestyles and family units to try to emulate. The nuclear family that is still held up by white men like Bush, Reagan, Moynihan, and pushed down our throats in TV programs year after year is not necessarily going to be a functional model for African Americans. It was not for my mother, my sister, my older brother, or me.

So, all this about, You have to have a man in the house, doesn't mean a thing to me. Sometimes, the first step in creating a functional family is to get that child molesting, womanizing, misogynist freak OUT of the house. I put that out especially to African American women because we have a harder time than other women achieving what is considered normal in this society. And a man is not the answer. We are the answer. When the family is a safe place for women and children, it is functional. When it is an agent of oppression—where our dreams die daily, where our asses are kicked, where our ambitions are thwarted and our children molested, where we are unpaid servants, where we are raped— it is dysfunctional. I don't care how it looks from the outside.

I don't hold my mother accountable for what my father did to me. I hold her accountable for what she did to me——she abandoned me. A parent's job is to protect their child. It's sad to think that that has to include protecting a child from her own father. One of the reasons I chose not to have children is because I knew being a perpetrator can be part of a victim's psychological make-up. I knew until I healed that I didn't have a right to bring another being into the world. I didn't have a right to end up in recovery groups saying, I'm sorry I abused my baby (or married someone who did). The decisions I made caused some pain in my life and are still a source of pain sometimes, but I decided not to reenact my parent's abuse and abandonment.

I work with young people, and I've had to learn how to deal with anger. My father would just "snap" when he got angry, and hit me. Well, I couldn't be around young people, "snapping." Kids, especially African American youngsters, have enough of that, of people knocking their brains out at home, and then going out in the street and getting beaten by the police. I wanted to be the kind of person that could help young people, not be another source of oppression. If my mother did the best she could, well, I have to say, it wasn't enough. Even under the most oppressive circumstances we sometimes have choices. One way out of remaining a victim is to make a conscious choice not to victimize yourself or others with less power than you.

DOROTHY ALLISON: My mother believed absolutely in family values. She was going to hang onto that family, and she thought that that was saving her girls from a worse fate. As a feminist, my purpose is to say, No. There are much better choices, and then to make those choices possible. The shelter movement in this country is still vastly inadequate and embattled. If you're trying to make it possible for women to live on their own and support their children, there's no funding for that. The funding available is to get them back home or to get women in another marriage. I worked with shelters in Washington D.C. and the biggest competitor was the Catholic Church. They wanted to heal the family. I'm not interested in healing the family. I'm interested in protecting children and making it possible for people to *get out* and get their own lives.

135

Right now, they're over there, the people that own those stories. I want to laugh. Why are you crying? That's fake. You just want donations. Take your loss like Latasha Harlins. We didn't cry when that Korean killed that girl. We felt bad, damn, why'd they kill her? Damn. We just took it as a loss. Turned our cheeks. But, then the Rodney King case, they said "Not Guilty" and we said, "Nah-nah, we can't turn the other cheek on this one 'cause we don't have no more cheeks. . . .

—from "Some People Don't Count," *The Village Voice*
(an article by Mark Cooper and Greg Golden, quoting a man they only identify as "Willie, a Los Angeles resident and looter")

136

STRANGE JUICE
(or the murder of Latasha Harlins)

1.

I remember my boyfriend, the dark behind the brown of his eyes and how he look in his leather. I was walking with that good feeling thinking about him, the next day of school—maybe I go, maybe I don't. You know who gives a fuck. And nothing special, you know nothing is so special except now I'm dead. It's the day I died. And the sky was red-brown gauze. You could see patches of blue if you look up but I don't hardly ever look up. My eyes on the ground checking out my feet in orange Reeboks. What else I remember? Now that I look back it seems like the collard greens piled up on plywood boards at the door was huge green tears that tried to warn me. The day was the same but different. I didn't do nothin'. I slid open the glass door of the refrigerator that keeps all the beverages cool, it's so hot here. My eyes glance up at the camera pointed like a gun from the corner of the wall. Fuck it. I slip the cold bottle of orange juice in my backpack, go to the counter. I'll get some gum, if she say something I'll say, aw bitch I was gonna buy this juice, you think I'm stupid. Wonder what we gonna do in school tomorrow. I be so glad to get out the ninth grade, go to high school. If I'm late for homeroom one more time—

"Oh bitch please! I was gonna pay for—OOG FU WOO SHIT SUE! Speak English hoe! Take your damn juice. I wasn't stealing nothin' from you chink ass hoe!"

She grabbed me. Bitch! I hit that hoe upside her jaw. Who the fuck she think she is putting her hands on somebody. Fuck this hoe, I ain' gon' argue with this bitch. I turn my back. And walk away. I see the collard greens again only now they're growing like big trees then I see a red dirt road in the middle of the salad bar, no lie, like I'm high or something. Then everything is normal Korea town fruit stand again. Del Monte corn out a can poured in a stainless steel tub, iceberg, romaine, bran muffins and brownies wrapped in clear plastic. Fuck it I'm not thirsty no way.

137

I don't hear the blast till I'm dead
I don't feel nothin' either
as I split in half
a dog yelps
and every sound I ever heard
flies out my mouth on green wings.
Crimson waterfalls open in my skull
and my bones come aloose,
The dog is screaming
like a siren now
and in a distance a bucket of water
spills over on a dusty red dirt road

and my heart quits
falls face first in
shattered glass on a
concrete floor.
The camera keeps
rolling.
My left leg twitches.
I don't cry.
Fifteen.
Green as greens
passing from sight
under broken bottles of light.

2.

I don't remember what I did
wrong.
Somebody hit you, you hit 'em back.
She didn't have to shoot me.
I was born here
and someone can shoot me and go home
and eat turkey on Thanksgiving—
what kinda shit is that?
Videotape the bitch killing me,
the hoe's own videotape
recording
the end of my days
reeling obscenely
for TV cameras—
my blood
sweet Jesus!
Rolling 20s

138

Bounty Hunters

PJs

Imperial Courts

NWA

LAPD

South Central

Hollywood

18th Street Diamond Riders

Easy Riders

it's a brown thing

it's a black thing

Crips

Bloods, Mexicans together forever tonight.

I don't remember . . .

I jus' wanted some juice

and now I'm dead.

Killed by a model minority

success story.

Listen, is anybody gonna

say anything?

I was gonna get a new orange leather jacket

to match my Reeboks.

I was passing math *and*

doing good in English.

Fuck history, I'm tired of hearing

bout George Washington

and Columbus.

I told that cracker, "Shit, mutherfucker

what about us?"

No, I *wasn't* pregnant,

but I was gonna have a baby,

definitely, one day.
I like Luther Vandross, Tone Loc
and Queen Latifa.
Listen, is anybody gonna
say anything?
Community service!
A white bitch
with a pink slit
between her legs
like mine,
drips red.
A white girl that probably got
into law school on the
affirmative action birthed
by black people's struggle,
sitting on a seat
that was opened up
for her by Rosa Parks and
Fannie Lou Hamer,
nig—no black people, African
Americans, like me, marching
under fire, hoses, broken glass
gasolined bodies
testicles sliced off,
strange fruit, tossed to dogs.
Swinging from trees.

This white judge woman
hooded in mahogany-walled
chambers decides my life
is not worth nothing.

A fifteen-year-old black girl
equals zero in this white bitch's book.
She sentences this yellow gunslinger
to community service and probation.
What are the terms of her probation,
that she don't kill nobody white?
Does anybody hear me?
Without my tongue.
Fifteen and out of time.
Listen to the gasoline on the wind.
Listen to my blood rhyme—
drip drop on the sidewalk.
Hear me children—
and BURN.

IN MY FATHER'S HOUSE

1.

together alone one night we were watching t.v.
& my father shot to his feet as "The Star Spangled Banner"
hailed the network's last gleaming.
he stood at attention saluting the red & white striped
tongue gyrating on the tv screen.
"Daddy," I said, "you don't have to do that."
"I know I don't have to but I want to," he said.

my mother slipped on her sweater & disappeared.
we rolled loose to corners of the room.
buttoned in cold; bones of children knitting shadows in the dark,
dreaming of pullovers, cardigans, cashmere & mohair.
"She never wanted children," he explained.

he told me his father put his foot on his neck
& beat him until his nose bled.
he left home when he was 14,
an Aries full of blind light
trying to wrap barbed wire around the wind.

my father bent a piece of rubber hose
into a black ellipse, then taped the ends together
to make a handle. he beat me with this.

I was grown, in my apartment,
when the cat sprang up on my record player
claws gouging Bob Marley's "Burnin' & Lootin'"
I snatched that cat off the record player

slammed it to the floor,
beat skin, teeth, skull with my fists,
tied its legs together & yanked its tail back
exposing the anus, tiny fist curled pink.
I picked up a burning cigarette from the ashtray
& started to stick it up that cat's asshole—
something stopped me.

spliced between the blind night of a forgotten scream
it would be ten years before I remembered
my father breaking open my asshole.
the memory would walk up behind me like bad news,
as unbelievable as Mayor Goode dropping a bomb on Osage Avenue,
as unbelievable as doctors betting on how much oxygen it would take
to blind a baby in an incubator then turning up the oxygen to see.
it would come like the nurse in the Tuskeegee syphilis night,
basket full on magic light, lies & placebos.
it would come counter-clockwise like bent swastikas.
it came just when I was learning to stand, to speak.
it grabbed me by my knees & dragged me down the years
stopping where I disappeared 35 years ago.

143

2.
we had a tree,
an avocado tree.
first my father painted it
then he killed it.
even before he decided
to cut the postage stamp-size
swimming pool
into the lawn,

he downed the tree.
I was gone then,
gone long & gone far.
but denial & amnesia
made me send father's day & birthday cards.
in one card I asked,
as I rarely did,
for something:
some avocados.
I said send me
some avocados
from the tree, Daddy.
I got $20 in the mail
& instructions to go
buy some avocados.
144   he didn't tell me
what he had done
to the tree.

3.
I say you raped me
you say it's a damn lie

you remember being a boy
running after rabbits in Texas
fast as the grass
tall as the sun

crazy slut of a life leaves you with 4 kids & no wife,
3 gone bad
I just like you:

an achiever
a star
a homeowner
a heterosexual
an athlete
who buys a Mercedes
for his wife & a Porsche
for himself.
a son shining
finally like you.

you fill the rooms
with him,
blue ribbons
& trophies fall
off the wall,
but strange whispers crawl
off the pages of the
local colored tabloid
to the *New York Times:*
they say
this youngest boy *rapes,*
humiliates women.
he is tried,
but acquitted—
you know how
women lie.

4.
at 14 I cooked, cleaned
no one asked how school was going,

what I needed or dreamed.
I had to have dinner ready at 5:30
biscuits cornbread ribs chicken meatloaf
I was cooking dinner one night
& my father offered to help me
as he sometimes did,
relieving me of some small task.
that night he offered to set the table.
the food was hot, ready to eat,
my little brother had just come in
from football practice,
I went to sit down at the table
& stopped shocked.
my father had only set a place
for himself & my little brother.

"I thought you had already eaten," he offered.
I made no move to get another plate,
neither did he.
he served his son
the food I had prepared.
they ate,
I disappeared,
like the truth
like the tree.

5.
I crawl from under
childhood's
dark table,
black tree
bleeding

spiralling to apogee,
broke doll yawning:
ma ma   ma ma
childhood consumed.
black moon
rising,
eating up
the sky,
a survivor—
heading home,
to my own house.

WILD THING

And I'm running,
running wild
running free,
like soldiers down
the beach,
like someone
just threw me
the ball.
My thighs pump
thru the air
like tires
rolling down
the highway
big & round
eating up the ground
of America
but I never been any
further than 42nd Street.
Below that is as
unfamiliar as my
father's face,
foreign as the smell of
white girls' pussy,
white girls on tv.
My whole world is
black & brown & closed,
till I open it
with a rock,

148

christen it with
blood.
BOP BOP
the music
pops thru me
like electric shocks,
my sweat is a
river running
thru my liver
green with hate,
my veins bulge out
like tomorrow,
my dick is
the Empire State Building,
I eat your fear
like a chimpanzee
ow ow
ow whee
ow!
My sneakers glide off
the cement like
white dreams
looking out at the world
thru a cage of cabbage
& my mother's fat,
hollering don't do this
& don't do that.
I scream against the restraint
of her big ass sitting on my face
drowning my dreams in sameness.

149

I'm scared to go
it hurts me to stay.
She sits cross legged
in front the tv
telling me no
feeding me
clothing me
bathing me in her ugliness
high high in the sky
18th floor of the projects.
Her welfare check buys me $85 sneakers
but can't buy me a father.
She makes cornbread from Jiffy box mix
buys me a new coat
$400, leather like everybody else's.
I wear the best man!
14 karat gold chain
I take off before I go wildin'.
Fuck you nigger!
Nobody touches my gold!
My name is Leroy
L-E-R-O-Y
bold gold
I got the goods
that make the ladies
yound & old
sign your name across my heart
I want you to be my baby
Rapper D
Rapper G
Rapper *I*

me me *me!*
my name is lightning
across the sky.
So what I can't read
you spozed to teach me
you the teacher
I'm the ape
black ape
in white sneakers
hah hah
I rape
rape
rape
I do the wild thing
I do the wild thing.
My teacher asks me
what would I do
if I had 6 months
to live.
I tell her I'd fuck her,
sell dope & do the wild thing.
My thighs are locomotives
hurling me thru the
underbrush of Central Park,
the jungle.
I either wanna be a cop
or the biggest dope dealer in Harlem
when I grow up.
I feel good!
It's a man's world,

my sound is king
I am the black man's sound.
Get off my face whining bitch!
No, I didn't go to school today
& I ain't goin' tomorrow!
I like how the sky looks
when I'm running,
my clothes are new & shiny,
my tooth gleams gold.
I'm fast as a wolf
I need a rabbit,
the sky is falling
calling my name
Leroy Leroy.
I look up

blood bust
in my throat
it's my homeboys
L.D., C.K. & Beanbutt!
Hey man what's up!
I got the moon
in my throat,
I remember when
Christ sucked my dick
behind the pulpit,
I was 6 years old,
he made me promise
not to tell no one.
I eat cornbread &
collard greens.

I only wear Adidas
I'm my own man,
they can wear New Balance or Nike
if they want,
I wear Adidas.
I'm L.D.
lover
mover
man with the money
all the girls know me.
I'm classified as mentally retarded
but I'm not
least I don't think
I am
Special Education classes
eat up my brain
like last week's greens
rotting in plastic containers.
My mother never
throws away anything.
I could kill her
I could kill her
all those years
all those years
I sat
I sat
I sat in classes
for the mentally retarded
so she could get
the extra money welfare gives

153

for retarded kids.
So she could get
some money
some motherfuckin' money.
That bitch
that bitch
I could kill her.
all those years
I sat next to kids
who shitted on themselves,
dreaming amid
rooms of dull eyes
that one day
my rhymes
would break open
the sky
& my name would
be written
across the marquee
at the Apollo
in bold gold
me bigger
than Run DMC
Rapper G
Rapper O
Rapper *Me*
"Let's go!" I scream.
My dick is a locomotive
my sister eats like a 50¢ hot dog.
I scream, "I *said* let's go!"

It's 40 of us
a black wall of sin.
The god of our fathers
descends down & blesses us,
I say thank you Jesus.
Now let's do the
wild thing.
I pop off the cement
like toast outta toaster
hot hard crumbling
running
running
the park is green
combat operation
lost soul
looking for Lt. Calley
Jim Jones
anybody who could direct
this spurt of semen
rising to the sky.
soldiers
flying thru
the rhythm
"Aw man!
nigger *please*
nigger
nigger
nigger,
I know
who I am."

My soul sinks
to its knees &
howls under the
moon rising full,
"Let's get a female jogger!"
I shout into the twilight
looking at the
middle class thighs
pumping past me,
cadres of bitches
who deserve to die
for thinking they're better
than me.
You ain't better than
nobody bitch.

The rock begs my hand
to hold it.
It says, "Come on man"
T.W., Pit Bull, J.D. & me
grab the bitch
ugly big nose white bitch
but she's beautiful 'cause she's white
she's beautiful 'cause she's skinny
she's beautiful 'cause she's gonna die
'cause her daddy's gonna cry
Bitch!
I bring the rock down
on her head
sounds dull & flat
like the time I busted

the kitten's head.
The blood is real & red
my dick rises.
I tear off her bra
feel her perfect pink breasts
like Brooke Shields
like the bitches in Playboy
Shit! I come all over myself!
I bring the rock down
the sound has rhythm
hip hop ain't gonna stop
till your face sees
what I see everyday
walls of blood
walls of blood
she's wriggling like
a pig in the mud.
I never seen a pig
or a cow
'cept on tv.
Her nipples are like
hard strawberries
my mouth tastes
like pesticide.
I fart.
Yosef slams her
across the face with a pipe.
My dick won't get
hard no more.
I bring the rock down

157

removing what she
looks like forever
ugly bitch
ugly bitch
I get up
blood on my hands
semen in my jeans
the sky is black
the trees are green
I feel good baby
I just did
the *wild thing!*

HUMAN TORSO GIVES BIRTH

I met her in *Jet Magazine* 10,000 years ago. The father of the baby preferred not to have his name known.

> eight to eighty
> blind, crippled or crazy
> a hard dick has no conscience
> (or embarrassment)
> men will stick their dick anywhere

I am not *anywhere*, she says. I am a person. It was a person he stuck his dick in. That hole between where legs shoulda been was not a cylindrical sphere of emptiness a falling pine knot left in a fence. I am not a hole in a fence. *Those* nights, all he wanted as I scooted over the sheets, my lips claiming his penis, my tongue his anus. He held my shoulders down and plunged into me like a tank rolling through town. I was a woman in a war zone, ravished and ready, surrounded by gun metal and singeing flesh.

Now he tells me it was a bad dream that made him ashamed.

But they can't take my baby from me. I won't let them she says determinedly. I am more fun than a circus as I show the judge how I can change a diaper with my teeth and tongue.

I dream of a bearded Japanese lover chasing me under the full moon. The moon is bleeding, my feet push off the sand and my legs are strong and swift. I hit the highway, blood pouring out the sky, my arms swinging as I run.

I dream of breaking bricks with my fists, turning flips and flying across the stage at Madison Square Garden. Black female 6th degree black belt, all the people screaming and cheering me on.

She stops talking and fumbles with her tongue trying to push the Velcro tabs of the diaper together. I move to help her. Her face dies when she

159

says thank you. I realize she has had to say thank you forever.

She sticks her tongue in the the baby's navel. It laughs. She rubs her head against its cheek. Looking at me she says with the fervor of the sea, "Maybe, my baby will be a samurai."

ONE DAY

All week my period plays at coming
then leaves me bewildered staring
in my panties at faint brown stains
I haven't seen in 30 years.
Is this the end? As it was in the
beginning (brown stains in cotton underwear)
so shall it be in the end?

It never crossed my mind it would hurt—
no long-legged daughters to hate me
or call me old fashioned or outta style
or to say like white girls on tv, "Gee Mom
you just don't understand," that it
would stretch my heart out
of shape like this, mark my smile
draw such rings under my eyes.
No one ever told me, I never knew
to be part of the counter culture
would be so lonely.

I felt for so long I had to save my own life,
no use in two of us drowning.
And then there was the ABUSE, how it left me
uncomfortable with a naked infant on my lap,
how I was afraid of descending down
to lick the little clitoris or of sticking
my finger up its vagina between diaper changes.
I mean this is what was done to me.

All my life the sound of a child crying
like fingernails raking down a blackboard
twisted something inside of me till it snapped
screaming: shut up shut up SHUT THE FUCK UP!
And I would want to slap, punch, stomp
throw it out the window or in a pot of boiling water—
anything! to get it to stop that
stop that goddam motherfucking crying!

Then I work.
I work years
in a circle
in a group
in a journal
alone.
I heave, crawl, vomit, abreact, 12 step, psycho-this, therapy
that, anger workshops, homeopathy, crystals—
all on poverty wages.

And I remember
a man so mean
so different from the face in photographs
and home movies.
I remember a woman with
red fingernails like razors
up my vagina.
I cry
shake
face the impossible,
write it
tell it.

I can't see any change.
Just all my time, money and
most of my youth spent,
and shelves of books: *The Best Kept Secret,*
Prisoners of Childhood, Kiss Daddy Goodnight,
The Courage to Heal, Father Daughter Incest.
Then one day the woman downstairs,
her with the dope smell escaping
from under the door's dark face,
takes in a baby for money.
And often under the deafening boom boom
of music so loud it sounds like a cannon
being fired I hear a baby crying.

One day it's just a crying and a crying
but instead of wanting to bash its head
on the sidewalk I relax, I relax all over
and a warm pink glow expands around my heart
like in some new age instruction book for meditation,
and I whisper, if that baby was mine
I would just hold it, hold it and hold it, 11 hours
if it took that long, till it stopped crying.
If that baby was mine I say slowly
and see the tiny child body safe in my warm brown arms.
If it was mine, I whisper again.
Maybe the baby hears me 'cause the crying
downstairs, in my soul, stops as I hold
my work, the work of a lifetime close to me.

163

IF YOU WERE LIKE THE HEROINE IN A COUNTRY AND WESTERN SONG

A Performance Script by Theory Girls

ANCHORWOMAN: America is teeming with angry women. The last few years have seen an incredible outbreak of female crime. In "Deadly Medicine," pediatric nurse Susan Ruttan kills children. In "The Rape of Dr. Willis," Jaclyn Smith murders the man who raped her. In "A Mother's Justice," Meredith Baxter is a mother obsessed with tracking down her daughter's rapist.

Things are looking up for the wild girls of the movies. In an encouraging trend, there have been a number of movies in the past year featuring the kind of bad girl roles all actresses covet. Women who kill are in. Women who whine are out.

165

Traci Lords is an enterprising L.A. policewoman who rids the streets of crime in "Intent to Kill." In "The Company of Darkness," Helen Hunt plays a rookie cop out to get a serial killer. In "It's Nothing Personal," Amanda Donahoe is an angry policewoman who becomes a professional killer.

Reality-based dramas that re-enact violence are in. Fantasy-based soap operas that fabricate romance are out. Female crisis-of-the-week movies are definitely in. Movies are always the product of a time and a place. The conflicts they ignite often reflect the most compelling controversies of an era.

And now, folks, let's meet some real victims. Today's topic is "Women Who Couldn't Leave Their Abusive Mates":

AILEEN: I was beaten with a gas can.

ARLENE: I was stalked with a tire iron and a sledgehammer.

AILEEN: I was stabbed in the leg with a hunting knife.

ARLENE: I was ordered to strip so he could flick hot cigarette ashes on my body.

AILEEN: I was stabbed.

ARLENE: I had a skull fracture.

AILEEN: I had skin torn off my face.

ARLENE: I was not allowed to leave the house.

AILEEN: I was not allowed to shower or to brush my teeth.

166

ARLENE: One time he slit my eye, and another time he broke my jaw.

AILEEN: He asked me for my wedding rings.

ARLENE: Without them they wouldn't be able to identify my body.

AILEEN: He said he could kill me easily.

ARLENE: And nothing would ever happen to him.

AILEEN: I knew that was true.

ARLENE: When the police came, he told them I was being emotional.

MRS. AMERICA: Excuse me!

ANCHORWOMAN: I believe we have a comment from the audience.

MRS. AMERICA: Yes. I was wondering, did you see when Susan Dey offed her physically abusive boyfriend in "Bed of Lies"? And when Dolly Parton offed her physically abusive boyfriend in "Wild Texas Wind"? I mean, why didn't you just kill them? There isn't a court in the world who would convict you for self-defense!

ANCHORWOMAN: That's a very interesting comment, Mrs. America. We'll hear more about how these women defended themselves in a moment. But first, a word from our sponsors:

Did you know that last year more than half of female murder victims in the US were slain by husbands or boyfriends? Yes, the proverbial war between the sexes is still raging. In fact, it's escalating! For example: Charles Stuart, a struggling fur salesman in Boston, murdered his pregnant wife, a lawyer, because he feared she was gaining the *upper hand*. Marc Lepine, an unemployed twenty-five-year-old engineer, gunned down fourteen women in a University of Montreal engineering classroom because they were *all a bunch of feminists*. But today's women fight back, as we shall see. Now, let's return to "Women Who Couldn't Leave Their Abusive Mates."

167

AILEEN: That night I told my boyfriend I was going to leave. He beat me for hours. He threatened to kill me and then kill himself.

ARLENE: He held a shotgun pointed right at my chest.

AILEEN: He said he didn't think he'd let me live until morning. I believed him. I shot him.

ARLENE: He said if he couldn't have me, no one could. When he was seven feet away I shot him.

AILEEN: He jumped, and I thought he was coming after me. So I just closed my eyes and kept pulling the trigger, over and over.

ARLENE: Yes!

MRS. AMERICA: Wait, wait wait! In "Wife, Mother, Murderer," which is a true story, by the way, Judith Light is a woman who murders her husband with arsenic to collect his life insurance. I hope your husbands had life insurance.

AILEEN: No, but at least he's dead. When my husband was alive, I couldn't walk out the door without permission to walk out the door.

ARLENE: When you love him and he puts his head in your lap and tells you how sorry he is, that he didn't mean to do it, not to hate him, you believe it will change. You want to believe it.

169

AILEEN: I never knew that my story was the same as every other person down the street.

MRS. AMERICA: No, no, no. Not like every other person, OK? No, this is just like "Two Women," you know, when Susan Lucci is an FBI agent who goes in search of a hitwoman who turns out to look just like her.

ANCHORWOMAN: Thank you, ladies, for sharing your tragic yet heartwarming stories with us tonight. And now, some late breaking news: Aileen Wuornos, thirty-three years old, a beer-drinking, chain-smoking prostitute, has been convicted of the slaying of Richard Mallory, and is suspected of murdering as many as seven middle-aged male motorists whose bodies were found alongside highways in central Florida. Evidence indicates that the men were lured to the isolated areas where they were subsequently shot repeatedly with small caliber bullets. All of the victims were robbed, and condom packages were left behind in several of the cars. News of the killings is spreading like wildfire from one woman's ear to another. But first, a word from our sponsors:

ANCHORWOMAN: Welcome back to "Infotainment Tonight"! Now, let's go live to the set of the new television movie based on the life of Aileen Wuornos. Let's watch. We enter the plot as Aileen sits in jail awaiting trial. She's talking to Arlene Pralle, a born-again Christian woman who sympathizes with Aileen and believes she can be saved.

ARLENE: Hello, Aileen? My name is Arlene Pralle. I'm born again. You're going to think I'm crazy, but Jesus told me to call you.

AILEEN: I don't know what you've heard. Whatever it is, it's all lies. How would anybody else know what happened to me? I was always by myself. The only one that knows this story is me, and I'll write the book.

MRS. AMERICA: Yeah, right. She'll write the book and they'll make the movie, because this is *an actual news event*. Another amazing story for prime time.

ARLENE: I was sitting in a hospital waiting room during my father's open heart surgery. I saw your picture in the paper. I read your story. And since that day, I've felt such a compassion deep within me for you.

AILEEN: Isn't that nice. *My* father was convicted of kidnapping and raping a child. He hung himself in prison. I'm glad, too. Motherfucking pervert deserved to die. I was abandoned when I was six months old.

ARLENE: I was adopted, too. I've always prayed for a sister. When I heard about your suicide attempts, my heart just went out to you. I have also tried to commit suicide.

AILEEN: I used to live in an old junked car in the woods. I hitchhiked everywhere, got raped, oh, maybe ten or twelve times.

ARLENE: I have also had a very stormy background.

AILEEN: I have been labeled as a serial killer, been framed by law enforcement as a serial killer. I'm no serial killer. I had no intention of killing anyone. I told you I was raped, and that is what happened in every case. Everybody's making money off me for books and movies. This is all a conspiracy.

MRS. AMERICA: I saw her on all of those shows: "Hard Copy," "Geraldo," and a "Current Affair." They said she was a Lesbian Killer, a Damsel of Death. I thought, *what on earth could have made her want to kill all those guys?*

AILEEN: I had lots of guys, ten or twelve a day. If I wanted to kill just anybody, I had lots of chances. If I am a so-called man-hater, I could have killed them all. But I didn't. I am really just a nice person.

171

ARLENE: Some people pick the darkness. But I don't think you are like that. When I first heard about your suicide attempts, and about your being a call girl and stuff, my heart just went out to you.

MRS. AMERICA: I saw a spread on these two in *Vanity Fair* and *Glamour* magazine, too. They were really milking this story. The headlines were totally sensational, like *Is she a hooker with a heart of gold? Or a killer who shook hands with the devil? Is she a maniac? Or just a woman evening the score?*

ARLENE: You are very kind and compassionate. You have a heart of gold.

ANCHORWOMAN: When it was discovered that Aileen had used the money stolen from her victims to support her female lover, Tyria Moore, Hollywood flipped.

You couldn't ask for a better real-life version of *Thelma and Louise*. As a seemingly sinister package of sex and violence—kinky, calculating, and lesbians to boot—their story will make the perfect television movie to satisfy the curiosity of women across the nation.

ARLENE: Lee, tell me about Tyria.

AILEEN: It was love beyond imaginable. Earthly words cannot describe how I felt about Tyria.

ARLENE: You were very caring. And, in spite of what she did, she cared about you.

AILEEN: I loved her. People don't understand the love. It wasn't a sexual thing. My love is a mental thing between me and Tyria. I loved her for who she was, although I didn't realize she had a two-faced heart.

173

ARLENE: But you still love her.

AILEEN: Yeah. I think maybe the cops threatened her, and said, "Look, you're gonna get first degree murder, you're gonna go to prison for the rest of your life, you might even go to Death Row with her."

ARLENE: She was afraid, Aileen. They used her as bait. But you protected her.

AILEEN: Of course. I loved her to the max. The only reason I confessed is because I loved her too much. I didn't want her to get into trouble because she isn't the one. I am the one.

ARLENE: And all that time Tyria thought that killing those men would change you. That one day you would get all your hatred out and you would change. I think what you want is to be smothered in love.

ANCHORWOMAN: What's so interesting about a female serial killer? In a recent *Glamour* magazine poll, prominently displayed next to a feature story on Aileen Wuornos, *Glamour* asked its readers: Do you believe that being beaten repeatedly can create such a state of hopelessness that murder is a woman's only way out? Eighty-eight percent say yes! *Glamour* asks, If such a woman kills her mate, should she be found not guilty? Eighty-one percent say yes! Should governors consider granting clemency to battered women imprisoned for murdering their mates? Eighty-three percent say yes! Would granting clemency encourage other women to kill their mates? Fifty-six percent say no—no woman kills a man after only one attack. It takes months, even years of abuse before it builds to murder.

Will public sympathy help Aileen Wuornos get out of her unfortunate predicament? Let's find out.

AILEEN: Am I supposed to die because I'm a prostitute? No, I don't think so. People don't understand how a prostitute can get raped! When a man rapes a woman, he assaults your whole body. He puts his penis down your throat, cramming it down your throat. He tears your hair out of your head. He beats your face in. He rips your asshole wide open. Prostitutes get raped all the time. I was raped.

MRS. AMERICA: After my divorce, I needed money so bad, I thought about stripping at one of those clubs. But I changed my mind after I saw Jodie Foster get gang-raped in *The Accused*.

AILEEN: He said he didn't have the money, and then he put a cord around my neck. He said, "You're going to do everything I say, bitch, or I'll kill you. I've done it before . . . Your body will still be warm for my huge cock. You want to die, slut?" I said I'd do what he said, and then he tied my hands to the steering wheel. He said he was gonna see how much meat he could pound up my ass. Then

174

he started having anal sex in a very violent manner. He said my crying turned him on, that he loved to hear my pain.

ARLENE: I keep thinking, there but by the grace of God I would be.

AILEEN: This guy was totally weird. He had a Visine bottle with alcohol in it which he squirted into my ass, my nose, and my vagina while he was doing his dirty deed. After he got off, he tried to strangle me. That's when I managed to get away. I got my gun. So the creep starts coming at me like this. And I said, "You better stop or I'm gonna keep shooting," and he wouldn't stop so I shot him, and he fell to the ground, and I shot him again.

ARLENE: You are like the heroine in a country and western song. Before I got born again, I was heavy into alcohol. I did things I'd rather not remember. I thought things. I was not a nice person.

175

MRS. AMERICA: That's all right my dear. Sometimes you have to let the anger out of you. You have to let loose your tension. Sometimes I feel like I'm just waiting to let it all out.

ARLENE: You are like me.

AILEEN: They all deserved it. They all asked for it. They shouldn't have been out there doing what they were doing. I told them thirty-seven times it was in self-defense.

ARLENE: I believe you. And I believe you are a harbinger of bigger things to come.

AILEEN: Sometimes when I think about what I've done I start feeling guilty. But then I think, maybe I'm a hero, because I am a killer of rapists. Anybody who rapes is, to me, a sick, deranged piece of puke who doesn't deserve to live.

MRS. AMERICA: You know, I think I was date-raped once. Right after my divorce I was really depressed and I met this guy in a bar who kept buying me drinks, and the next thing I remember I'm completely drunk, in bed with him . . . I got pregnant, and I had to have an abortion. I felt just like Sigourney Weaver in *Aliens*, you know, when she had that monster coming out of her belly.

ARLENE: You are the victim of an unfair society.

AILEEN: People keep choking me to death saying, "Hey, you're a prostitute, we want you to die, we don't give a damn, you know, we're gonna make a whole lotta money off you, we don't care about you, and you're almost dead," and all this other shit. I'm pissed. When you rape a whore it's called stealing. All I wanted was to get my money for sex. If I could do it clean, no problem.

176

ARLENE: If you are the first woman serial killer, you have reason to be.

MRS. AMERICA: Wait. Not so fast. I know you were abused as a child, and maybe you need therapy. But you've got to draw the line somewhere. I mean, I wanted to kill that guy who raped me, but I didn't go out and do it. You were out of control.

AILEEN: I didn't think I was out of control. I thought to myself, these men are out of control. I'm sick and tired of those men out there thinking they can control us, do whatever they damn well please with our bodies, and they think they can get away with it, 'cause this is a male dominant society, and *we're gonna treat you the way we want to, abuse you, destroy you. It doesn't matter to us, 'cause we can get away with it.*

ARLENE: If the world could know the real Aileen Wuornos, there's not a jury in the world that would convict you.

AILEEN: I am not a man-hater, don't you see? They're trying to make me look like a creep. I'm not a verbal or physical fighter. I like to be tranquil and at ease and enjoy life. I'm a decent person.

ARLENE: You are very beautiful, caring, and loving. You have become my life. It's as though a part of me were trapped in that jail with you. Our souls are bound together.

AILEEN: They're going to electrocute me, and I don't deserve it.

MRS. AMERICA: Oh, this is really stupid. So, everybody gets off on her story, and then they have no use for her. As usual, she gets it in the end. Just like Glenn Close in *Fatal Attraction*. That was a really good movie, except for the ending.

177

ANCHORWOMAN: Today's movies reflect the widespread fear that women, released from traditional restraints, will turn to unbridled *evil, mayhem,* and *murder.* This fear has turned out to be justified. We are awash in a sea of emancipated crime. The evidence is everywhere.

Last year, in the "Year of the Woman," vengeful Patricia Bowman, soon after she was raped by William Kennedy Smith, put on a Madonna T-shirt bearing the slogan, "I think (therefore) I am a sexual threat."

Vengeful women old and young put I Believe You Anita bumper stickers on their cars. Spoke out about date rapists. Worried about the loss of reproductive choice. Read books like *The Beauty Myth* and *Backlash.* Voted for anything in skirts.

Vengeful female TV viewers preferred killer women films to sexy soaps and disease-of-the-week weepers.

Perhaps we should consider the possibility that Hollywood sees a potentially vengeful audience more clearly than we see ourselves, that it sees an audience in an advanced state of denial, not unlike a drunk on a bar stool.

If this were a TV movie of the '70s or '80s, the woman would end up getting counseling and resolving her feelings. But here, when the subject of counseling comes up, she yells, "I don't need help. I need justice."

AILEEN: You are the only one, the only one who ever listened to me. I can die happy in that knowledge.

ARLENE: Don't give up honey. I'll tell your story to the world. I'll tell Geraldo and Oprah and the judge. We'll make "God Save Aileen" T-shirts. We'll spread the Word.

179

AILEEN: Forget it, Arlene. I am a nonentity prostitute. I disgust people. No one wants to defend me. I want to die, and quickly.

ARLENE: But until now, neither one of us really knew what love was like.

AILEEN: I love you. I will always love you. I hope I see you in heaven.

ARLENE: You and I are like Jonathan and David in the Bible. We made a covenant. We always know what the other is thinking and feeling. I just wish I was Houdini—I would get you out of there. If there was a way, I would do it, and we could go and be vagabonds forever.

AILEEN: Did you know that I am going to die in the same electric chair that killed

Ted Bundy. Now, isn't that ironic.

ARLENE: If you die, I will die. I'll just close my eyes, think about my friends and lovers, and it will just happen. Easy. I want you to go first, because I can never give you up until you're safely home.

AILEEN: I prayed to find someone like you.

ARLENE: I keep your letters in a red water cooler next to my shotgun.

180

A COMPLETE LIST OF PARTICIPANTS AT THE FEMINISM, ACTIVISM & ART CONFERENCE, NOVEMBER 6-8, 1992:

Curators: Laura Brün, Margaret Crane, Minnette Lehmann, Rupert Jenkins, Amy Scholder, Christine Tamblyn

Dorothy Allison
Cheryl C. Brodie
Shirley Carter
Christine Cobaugh
Wanda Coleman
Janet Dodson
Leslie Ernst
Jeanne Finley
Scarlot Harlot
Anne Healy
Osa Hidalgo-de la Riva
Andrea Juno
Yolanda López
Sue Martin
Susan McWhinney
Laura Miller
Irene Perez
Melissa Pokorny
Michelle Rollman
Dee Russell
Sapphire
Elizabeth Sisco
Diane Tani

181

Presented in conjuction with the Feminism, Activism & Art conference:

Big Butt Girls, Hard Headed Women
> A Performance by Rhodessa Jones

The Only Witness: Sexual Abuse and the Artist's Life
> A Performance by Dorothy Allison and Margeaux

A Life in Progress
> A Poetry Reading by Sapphire

Many Women Involved
> A Performance by Carla Kirkwood

If You Were like the Heroine in a Country and Western Song
> A Performance by Theory Girls

A video program in conjunction with the conference, Feminism, Activism & Art:

Curator: Cecilia Dougherty

Lutz Bacher: *My Penis*

Lucretia Bermudez: *Raid on a Peruvian Lesbian Bar*

Abigail Child: *Perils*

Hrafnhildur Gunnarsdottir/Sue Marcoux: *No Means Know*

Osa Hidalgo-de la Riva: *Mujeria: The Olmeca Rap*

Dee Russell/Scarlot Harlot: *Yes Means Yes. No Means No*

G.B. Jones/Jena von Brucker: *People in Your Neighborhood*

Lisa Mann: *Seven Lucky Charms*

Crystal Mason: *Was it Good for You?*

Jennifer Montgomery: *Tentacles*

Azian Nurudin: *Bitter Strength: Sadistic Response Version*

Ursula Purrer: *(untitled)*

Lisa Rudman: *excerpts from Women Political Prisoners in the US*

Leslie Singer: *Safe*

Valerie Soe: *Picturing Oriental Girls: A (Re)Educational Videotape*

CONTRIBUTORS NOTES

Dorothy Allison is the author of *Bastard out of Carolina* (Dutton/Plume), which was nominated for the National Book Award; *Trash* (Firebrand); and *The Women Who Hate Me* (Firebrand). She lives in the Bay Area.

Laura Brün is an interdisciplinary artist, writer, and the Executive Director of The LAB Gallery of San Francisco. She is currently working on an installation called "American Female."

Cheryl Cecile Brodie is a visual and performance artist. Her work often stems from her own life experience while resonating with the history of women and contemporary gender issues. She earned her degree in Interdisciplinary Art at San Francisco State University.

183

Christine Cobaugh is a visual artist, feminist and activist. She has been involved with the movement to end violence against women for eight years. She lives in the Bay Area.

Wanda Coleman is a poet, fiction writer, essayist, and recording artist. She has published six books, including *Hand Dance* and *African Sleeping Sickness* (both by Black Sparrow Press). She lives in Los Angeles.

Margaret Crane is a Bay Area writer. Since 1985, she has collaborated with photographer Jon Winet on over fifty exhibitions, performances and publications. They have recently completed a set of trading cards, "The Days of Our Lives," addressing social issues and featuring Marin County-based social service agencies.

Janet Dodson's work explores the various narratives of domestic life produced by mass media. *Family Values*, a video which explores the portrayal of Dagwood Bumstead as victim, and *Audience*, a video which analyzes the testimony of talk show participants from the point-of-view of the attendant audience, are her recent works.

Leslie Ernst is an installation artist and writer. Her current projects include *The Big Sweep*, a collaborative photonovella noir concerning labor struggles in Los Angeles; and *Hirsute*, an interactive photographic installation about social taboos related to women's body hair. She lives in Los Angeles.

Jeanne C. Finley is an independent video producer who also works as the Associate Dean of Film and Video at the California College of Arts and Crafts. She is currently working with Gretchen Stoeltje on an experimental documentary videotape about an American/Russian matchmaking service. In January, 1994, she will be the artist-in-residence in Istanbul, Turkey.

184

Rupert Jenkins is Associate Director of SF Camerawork. He curated *Murder as Phenomena* for Camerawork in 1992 and, with filmmakers Chris Beaver and Judy Irving, is currently curating an exhibition of photographs by the late Japanese photographer Yosuke Yamahata.

Carla Kirkwood is a writer/performer and public art collaborator. Her work includes *Woyzeck and Maria on East 94*, an interdisciplinary performance piece on women who murder; *There Are 206 Bones in the Human Body*, about torture in El Salvador; and a new work, *Bodies of Evidence*. She lives in San Diego, California.

Yolanda López is a visual artist, actively creating new images for Chicanas. She teaches painting at the University of California at Berkeley, and serves on the San Francisco Art Institute Artists Committee.

Sue Martin is an activist and artist who has worked in the field of violence against women for over 17 years. She teaches expressive arts for women with a special focus on healing from abuse. She is on the staff of the Family Violence Prevention Fund, a national public policy and education organization, and of the Tamalpa Institute. She is the co-author of *Domestic Violence, A Training Curriculm for Law Enforcement.*

Susan McWhinney is an artist and writer living in Brooklyn, New York.

Dee Russell is a performing artist, writer, director, and an American Film Institute Award-winning filmmaker. She just released a movie about gentrification in San Francisco called *Haight Street Poster Wars.* In 1994, she will make more films and perform internationally.

Sapphire is a poet, fiction writer, and performance artist. Her book, *American Dreams,* is forthcoming in January, 1994. Her work has been published in *Women on Women, HIGH RISK 2, Queer City: The Portable Lower East Side,* and *City Lights Review.* She lives in New York.

185

Elizabeth Sisco has participated in a series of five collaborative public art projects about San Diego (1988-1992). She has received grants from the National Endowment for the Arts, the California Arts Council, and Art Matters, Inc. She is a professor at Southwestern College in Chula Vista, California.

Theory Girls aka Laura Brün and Jennie Currie are both artists and writers who have presented numerous interdisciplinary performances and installations in the US since 1986. They mine popular culture for source material to recontextualize in critical and often humorous feminist interpretations of social and political issues that affect women.

CITY LIGHTS PUBLICATIONS

Acosta, Juvenal, ed. LIGHT FROM A NEARBY WINDOW: Poems of Contemporary Mexico
Allen, Roberta. AMAZON DREAM
Angulo de, Jaime. INDIANS IN OVERALLS
Angulo de, G. & J. JAIME IN TAOS
Artaud, Antonin. ARTAUD ANTHOLOGY
Bataille, Georges. EROTISM: Death and Sensuality
Bataille, Georges. THE IMPOSSIBLE
Bataille, Georges. STORY OF THE EYE
Bataille, Georges. THE TEARS OF EROS
Baudelaire, Charles. INTIMATE JOURNALS
Baudelaire, Charles. TWENTY PROSE POEMS
Bowles, Paul. A HUNDRED CAMELS IN THE COURTYARD
Broughton, James. COMING UNBUTTONED
Broughton, James. MAKING LIGHT OF IT
Brown, Rebecca. ANNIE OAKLEY'S GIRL
Brown, Rebecca. THE TERRIBLE GIRLS
Bukowski, Charles. THE MOST BEAUTIFUL WOMAN IN TOWN
Bukowski, Charles. NOTES OF A DIRTY OLD MAN
Bukowski, Charles. TALES OF ORDINARY MADNESS
Burroughs, William S. THE BURROUGHS FILE
Burroughs, William S. THE YAGE LETTERS
Cassady, Neal. THE FIRST THIRD
Choukri, Mohamed. FOR BREAD ALONE
CITY LIGHTS REVIEW #2: AIDS & the Arts
CITY LIGHTS REVIEW #3: Media and Propaganda
CITY LIGHTS REVIEW #4: Literature / Politics / Ecology
Cocteau, Jean. THE WHITE BOOK (LE LIVRE BLANC)
Codrescu, Andrei, ed. EXQUISITE CORPSE READER
Cornford, Adam. ANIMATIONS
Corso, Gregory. GASOLINE
Daumal, René. THE POWERS OF THE WORD
David-Neel, Alexandra. SECRET ORAL TEACHINGS IN TIBETAN BUDDHIST SECTS
Deleuze, Gilles. SPINOZA: Practical Philosophy
Dick, Leslie. KICKING
Dick, Leslie. WITHOUT FALLING
di Prima, Diane. PIECES OF A SONG: Selected Poems
Doolittle, Hilda (H.D.) NOTES ON THOUGHT & VISION
Ducornet, Rikki. ENTERING FIRE
Duras, Marguerite. DURAS BY DURAS
Eberhardt, Isabelle. THE OBLIVION SEEKERS
Eidus, Janice. VITO LOVES GERALDINE
Fenollosa, Ernest. CHINESE WRITTEN CHARACTER AS A MEDIUM FOR POETRY
Ferlinghetti, Lawrence. PICTURES OF THE GONE WORLD
Ferlinghetti, Lawrence. SEVEN DAYS IN NICARAGUA LIBRE
Finley, Karen. SHOCK TREATMENT
Ford, Charles Henri. OUT OF THE LABYRINTH: Selected Poems
Franzen, Cola, transl. POEMS OF ARAB ANDALUSIA
García Lorca, Federico. BARBAROUS NIGHTS: Legends & Plays
García Lorca, Federico. ODE TO WALT WHITMAN & OTHER POEMS
García Lorca, Federico. POEM OF THE DEEP SONG
Gil de Biedma, Jaime. LONGING: SELECTED POEMS
Ginsberg, Allen. HOWL & OTHER POEMS
Ginsberg, Allen. KADDISH & OTHER POEMS
Ginsberg, Allen. REALITY SANDWICHES
Ginsberg, Allen. PLANET NEWS
Ginsberg, Allen. THE FALL OF AMERICA
Ginsberg, Allen. MIND BREATHS
Ginsberg, Allen. PLUTONIAN ODE
Goethe, J. W. von. TALES FOR TRANSFORMATION
Hayton-Keeva, Sally, ed. VALIANT WOMEN IN WAR AND EXILE

Herron, Don. THE DASHIELL HAMMETT TOUR: A Guidebook
Herron, Don. THE LITERARY WORLD OF SAN FRANCISCO
Higman, Perry, tr. LOVE POEMS FROM SPAIN AND SPANISH AMERICA
Jaffe, Harold. EROS: ANTI-EROS
Jenkins, Edith. AGAINST A FIELD SINISTER
Kerouac, Jack. BOOK OF DREAMS
Kerouac, Jack. POMES ALL SIZES
Kerouac, Jack. SCATTERED POEMS
Lacarrière, Jacques. THE GNOSTICS
La Duke, Betty. COMPANERAS
La Loca. ADVENTURES ON THE ISLE OF ADOLESCENCE
Lamantia, Philip. MEADOWLARK WEST
Laughlin, James. SELECTED POEMS: 1935-1985
Le Brun, Annie. SADE: On the Brink of the Abyss
Lowry, Malcolm. SELECTED POEMS
Mackey, Nathaniel. SCHOOL OF UDHRA
Marcelin, Philippe-Thoby. THE BEAST OF THE HAITIAN HILLS
Masereel, Frans. PASSIONATE JOURNEY
Mayakovsky, Vladimir. LISTEN! EARLY POEMS
Mrabet, Mohammed. THE BOY WHO SET THE FIRE
Mrabet, Mohammed. THE LEMON
Mrabet, Mohammed. LOVE WITH A FEW HAIRS
Mrabet, Mohammed. M'HASHISH
Murguía, A. & B. Paschke, eds. VOLCAN: Poems from Central America
Murillo, Rosario. ANGEL IN THE DELUGE
Paschke, B. & D. Volpendesta, eds. CLAMOR OF INNOCENCE
Pasolini, Pier Paolo. ROMAN POEMS
Pessoa, Fernando. ALWAYS ASTONISHED
Peters, Nancy J., ed. WAR AFTER WAR (City Lights Review #5)
Poe, Edgar Allan. THE UNKNOWN POE
Porta, Antonio. KISSES FROM ANOTHER DREAM
Prévert, Jacques. PAROLES
Purdy, James. THE CANDLES OF YOUR EYES
Purdy, James. IN A SHALLOW GRAVE
Purdy, James. GARMENTS THE LIVING WEAR
Purdy, James. OUT WITH THE STARS
Rachlin, Nahid. MARRIED TO A STRANGER
Rachlin, Nahid. VEILS: SHORT STORIES
Reed, Jeremy. RED-HAIRED ANDROID
Rey Rosa, Rodrigo. THE BEGGAR'S KNIFE
Rey Rosa, Rodrigo. DUST ON HER TONGUE
Rigaud, Milo. SECRETS OF VOODOO
Ruy Sánchez, Alberto. MOGADOR
Saadawi El, Nawal. MEMOIRS OF A WOMAN DOCTOR
Sawyer-Lauçanno, Christopher, tr. THE DESTRUCTION OF THE JAGUAR
Scholder, Amy, ed. CRITICAL CONDITION: Women on The Edge of Violence
Sclauzero, Mariarosa. MARLENE
Serge, Victor. RESISTANCE
Shepard, Sam. MOTEL CHRONICLES
Shepard, Sam. FOOL FOR LOVE & THE SAD LAMENT OF PECOS BILL
Smith, Michael. IT A COME
Snyder, Gary. THE OLD WAYS
Solnit, Rebecca. SECRET EXHIBITION: Six California Artists
Sussler, Betsy, ed. BOMB: INTERVIEWS
Takahashi, Mutsuo. SLEEPING SINNING FALLING
Turyn, Anne, ed. TOP TOP STORIES
Tutuola, Amos. FEATHER WOMAN OF THE JUNGLE
Tutuola, Amos. SIMBI & THE SATYR OF THE DARK JUNGLE
Valaoritis, Nanos. MY AFTERLIFE GUARANTEED
Wilson, Colin. POETRY AND MYSTICISM
Wilson, Peter Lamborn. SACRED DRIFT
Zamora, Daisy. RIVERBED OF MEMORY